The Cinematic VR Formula

For B + J + A

The Cinematic VR Formula

by Chuck Ian Gordon

Proofreading by Jeremy Ratcliffe

Version 1.0a_final_en

http://www.cinematic-vr-formula.com

The German National Library (Deutsche Nationalbibliothek) holds data about this book accessible via internet at: http://dnb.dnb.de/

Imprint

The Cinematic VR Formula
A Beginner's Guide to Creating VR Movies

by Chuck Ian Gordon

English Proofreading by Jeremy Ratcliffe

Order information: http://www.cinematic-vr-formula.com

ISBN: 978-3-944218-10-6 eBook Version

ISBN: 978-3-944218-11-3 Print Version

Publisher: Gordon's Arcade™
Triftstr. 30, D-61350 Bad Homburg, Germany
CEO: Chuck Ian Gordon
http://www.GordonsArca.de/

Cover image: by Chuck Ian Gordon
Interior Images: By Chuck Ian Gordon and Fabian Schempp

Table of Contents

Foreword

Virtual Reality is a hype now in early 2017, Augmented Reality soon will be. Neither will stay a hype, but both will change our world in profound ways, as there are almost unlimited subjects to cover for VR and AR. However, this book focuses on Cinematic Virtual Reality and partly on Cinematic Augmented Reality. A blend of both characteristics is in the process of creating a whole new form of immersive entertainment bringing a new wonderland to our everyday lives.

As motion pictures took their first careful steps at the dawn of the 20th century creators had an awful lot to learn. The first movies didn't have cuts, moving cameras, closeups or stories. Look how movies evolved over time until today - wow! Now we are taking the same first careful steps in VR movie making.

As you read these lines you are one of those pioneers of VR movies - as Georges Méliès was a century ago with his unforgotten short movie: "A Trip to the Moon". This book is designed to act as - let's say - a collection of unstructured checklists for you to stay aware of the several subjects relevant to VR movie making. We have already learned a lot about VR movie making during the past few years and we will continue to do so, so this work can neither be complete nor finished.

I am not focusing on the latest hype technology like the VR goggles of company X and how to include the game engine drivers for it. Rather we will look at principles.

However, this book does make some bold predictions about future that might come in handy for you if you work on long term projects.

These design aspects should help make this book more useful for a longer period of time.

The Cinematic VR Formula

One last thing. I believe VR and AR will change our perception of the world and its underlying IT systems completely. However, VR won't replace traditional movies as they still have lots of advantages. But it will enrich our entertainment world and open bright new horizons. So, let's boldly film where no one has immersed us before!

Yours Chuck Ian Gordon
January 3rd 2017

P.S. Some parts of the book quote later developments up until September 2017 as it went through an early access phase and a longer editing process. So, don't worry about that. I don't have a time machine - yet.

Part I

What this book is not about

Before I tell you what this book is about let's have a quick look at what it is not about. It is not about movie making in general, about framing, staging or about digital production pipelines. For all of this there are excellent resources and I definitely recommend that you have a look at them because they really help you develop your movie making skills. This book is solely an addon to your movie making skills for VR movie making, so here are some reading tips if you want to develop your general movie making skills (I have read these myself).

The Writers Journey Mythic Structure for Writers - by Christopher Vogler

Film Directing Shot by Shot Visualizing from Concept to Screen (Michael Wiese Productions) - by Steven D. Katz

Framed Ink Drawing and Composition for Visual Storytellers Paperback – by Marcos Mateu-Mestre

Production Pipeline Fundamentals for Film and Games - by Renee Dunlop

As VR evolves at high speed I also recommend following the VR and AR news on the web. As of today, just a few weeks can fundamentally change the game.

Some great sources are http://uploadvr.com from Robert Scoble, http://roadtovr.com , http://vrscout.com , http://www.vrfocus.com , https://www.wearvr.com and in German http://vrodo.de

Enjoy reading and exploring!

Approach to this book and thanks

When I come across a subject that is interesting to me but which I have little knowledge about the first two things I do are: give a speech and/or write a book about it. This may sound crazy but it has proven to work very well for me. Reason 1 is: I explore the subject and really get to be an expert on various topics within it. Reason 2: as I know professionals will read this I put more effort in research and experimenting as I know my judges will expect good content. Reason 3: I get into contact with many interesting people who are experts and I learn from each of them a tiny bit. In the end when the book is published and I look back at what I have done I often realize that I have enhanced my skills profoundly. So, I encourage you to consider doing the same because in the two years of making this book I learned an awful lot.

Well, I didn't start from zero. I did my first computer graphics back in the 1980s on a C64 with Basic and Assembler. In the late 1980s, I did my first 3D graphics on an Atari ST and in 1998 I created my first Enterprise VR world. Wow. Sounds great, right? Well, unfortunately as we know today – the market didn't skyrocket back then. I produced VRML based (Virtual Reality Modeling Language) virtual worlds generated out of an Oracle database - a kind of mini second life you could say - 9 years before the great second life hype in 2007. Meanwhile I earned my money as an ordinary IT consultant and science fiction author. Written 2010 to 2011 my science fiction novel GameW0rldz was published in 2012 first in German, later in English (http://www.GameW0rldz.com). Actually, it is a novel about Virtual Reality (and some more stuff). In August 2012 I decided to dive deeper into modern 3D animation and started working on the 3futurez holodeck musical (http://www.3futurez.com). Then destiny struck. On 1st of September 2012 Palmer Luckey raised more than 2 million dollars for his Oculus Rift which was acquired by Facebook in 2014 for 2.3 billion dollars. This changed the world and all the industry. So, I suddenly found myself surrounded by an exploding VR technology industry, and I already had taken some important steps. In May 2015 at FMX I decided to write this book: "The Cinematic VR Formula" as I would need it for my holodeck musical production pipeline anyway. I also worked on new topics related to my IT career like "Virtual Reality Analytics" and co-authored a book about it (https://www.amazon.com/Virtual-Reality-Analytics-Business-Intelligence/dp/3944218094).

But since I hadn't created a Hollywood blockbuster yet I had to get some information and input from industry professionals from VR and movies. So, I just contacted many people and asked them if they would conduct an interview with me for my book: "The Cinematic VR Formula". And you know what? Many of them said yes. After creating my first VR works I also gave some speeches about VR movie making - for example at the Immersed Europe in September 2015 in Murcia, Spain, meeting professionals again. Co-founding our local VR meetup in Frankfurt Germany I added more interesting contacts and information to my list. The result, written down in this book is a collection of my own experience with creating 3D and VR, many of my own experiments, including those that caused me motion sickness, plus the structured experience of many professionals and enthusiasts of the VR and movie industry. Rather than publishing the interviews in a meeting-minutes-style I wrote summaries of the input I collected from the contributors. I intend to use this book like a collection of checklists for myself and hope it helps you to get a quick and structured collection of guidelines for your VR movie creation. Please let me know when you have produced something great! And also let me know if something ended in a disaster but you learned an important lesson from it. Either we succeed or we learn.

Another important thing is to have some fun. As I am a great fan of the 1980s Video Arcade days I structured this book like an 8-bit arcade videogame and also produced some 8-bit 3D illustrations for it. So, we will get our mission and advance through the different levels like raising money, planning the story, preproduction, production and postproduction to the grand finale of our release date and then some more.

Finally, it is time to say thank you. First to my family for leaving me the time to finish this book. Next, thanks for the wonderful input I got from so many unnamed people. Special thanks go to Nick Pittom, Director of <u>Firepanda Ltd</u>[1] who won the VR Jam with his great VR experience Collosse, to Brad Herman formerly Head of Dreamlab at Dreamworks (now co-founder of Spaces.com) for his wealth of valuable information and to my first interview partner Sabine Koder, filmmaker, writer and director, who helped me with starting this book. Also thanks to Fabian Schempp for some great 8-bit 3D models. And of course, to Palmer Luckey and Mark Zuckerberg who restarted the VR hype again and kickstarted the whole industry to provide us with amazing, improved VR technology.

And now: INSERT COINS... to read the next chapter ;-)

VR: History, Status, Future

History of Virtual Reality

Virtual reality is not a new thing. What storytellers thousands of years ago were able to create in the listeners' minds could be called virtual reality. One's imagination creates other worlds that the storytellers described. Later we were able to separate the stories from the people, telling them by using books. A book could wait a long time after the author was dead, and then somebody picked up that book and recreated the world he'd read about in his mind. I would definitely call this virtual reality. And it is a form of art that should and will be around for a long time in the future.

But when we come to more technical adaptions of virtual reality there are some major developments worth noting.

---

[1] http://www.firepanda.co.uk/

The Cinematic VR Formula

The 1935 short novel "Pygmalion's Spectacles" from Stanley Grauman Weinbaum.[2]

The 1939 View Master[3] - a stereoscopic analog device operated by disks using daylight. I got one myself in my childhood in the 1970s and still today it is absolutely great.

Then the famous Sensorama[4] from the 1950s and 1960s invented by Morton Heilig. It was a kind of arcade machine you could sit in front of and let yourself immerse with a stereo movie, stereo sound and smells.

In 1968 Ivan Sutherland created the "Sword of Damocles[5]". I would rather call it an early Augmented Reality Device that displayed simple 3D objects dependent on the head movement of the user. The movement was measured by strings from the ceiling and it was a huge apparatus that inspired the name.

In the 1990s there was the first major Virtual Reality wave trying to address the mass market which obviously failed. Prices were too high; the technology wasn't sophisticated enough. One example of this failure was the Nintendo Virtual Boy. Many of those developments were inspired by the VR film: "The Lawnmower Man" with Pierce Brosnan. Many of the technologies on the market we see today were anticipated back then in the movie.

Also the advent of the world wide web as we know it today played an important role. In 1994 Dave Raggett submitted a paper called "Extending WWW to support Platform Independent Virtual Reality" to the first world wide web conference. This led to VRML - the Virtual Reality (Markup/Modeling) language. I created my

---

[2] http://www.gutenberg.org/files/22893/22893-h/22893-h.htm

[3] https://en.wikipedia.org/wiki/View-Master

[4] https://en.wikipedia.org/wiki/Sensorama

[5] https://en.wikipedia.org/wiki/The_Sword_of_Damocles_(virtual_reality)

first interactive database generated VR worlds in 1998. The technology was amazingly developed providing spatial sound, animation, and programmability by Java and Javascript. There were various browser plugins - my favorite was the Cosmo Player originally by Silicon Graphics. Unfortunately, it was sold several times and not kept up to date, and as the technology wasn't ready many years passed and VR was used mainly by the military and by large companies, like in the car industry, with the necessary budget for high end VR installations. VR Caves were an alternative to VR headsets.

Status of Virtual Reality 2016/2017

With the development from 2012 to 2016 the whole industry restarted itself inspired - or driven - by Palmer Luckey with his Kickstarter success for Oculus and by Facebook who acquired Oculus later for 2.3 billion dollars.

Today we are in a very interesting phase of transition again. VR headsets have become widely available at affordable prices with solid to good technology. So many people started experimenting with VR, creating great demos and the first great games for virtual reality. People started asking whether and how this medium can be used for movies - for cinematic VR. There was a shift from 2015 where everybody at the FMX in Stuttgart talked about storytelling in VR (www.fmx.de). In 2016 the subject evolved to world building. It was not about storytelling but about creating experience space and letting users decide for themselves what they want to see and what not. Instead of linear stories, branched stories or simulations are the challenge for the creatives. We see subjects merge and fusions of the movie industry and the game industry. This process is ongoing right now in 2017.

Also there is lots of movement in the recording and display sector. Companies like Magic Leap with a funding budget of around 1.5 billion dollars (roughly half a billion from Google) are secretly working on possibly revolutionary light field display technology. Light field display technology (e.g. www.real-eyes.eu) in general is fascinating but has some steps to go still. With sufficient progress I would see it as the optimal immersive technology as it allows me to create a fully immersive dome or sphere to immerse me and other spectators to give us a 360°x180° surround VR experience without glasses - yes this would be a holodeck. All the technology components are there, and each of them just needs linear improvements not a quantum leap. So, I wouldn't even call this technology science fiction anymore but only speculate about the time it arrives in the mainstream. Imagine this real holodeck. Or imagine a tunnel to walk through in the subway to totally immerse you. You see an ad for beer while the lady next to you sees an ad for a new handbag and the guy next to her safely checks his account balance without anybody else being able to sneak a look because it is projected into his eyes only by backlit lenses or possibly by laser projection directly into his eyes.

At FMX 2016 Lytro showed the Lytro Cinema - a light field movie camera that can substitute a very high percentage of the ordinary movie production pipeline with its product in combination with Nuke - a 3D compositing software from the Foundry (who also launched their VR production product CaraVR). Lytro also announced the Lytro Immerge - a ball shaped light field camera for capturing live action light fields. (Well we were able to see the first prototype meanwhile and it is more a 1-by-1-meter array of plenoptic single cameras - nevertheless look at the results of their Halleluja video - we are on the way.) Not to forget the announcement of <u>Facebook and Otoy also working on volumetric video</u>[6] - the material we can see today is quite impressive. These or similar technologies have the potential to completely change the way we record, process and consume movies. So, the future of VR movies promises to be quite complex and at the same time very exciting! Let's close with a quote I love (for which it is controversially discussed whether it really is from Albert Einstein): "More than the past I am interested in the future as I intend to spend the rest of my life in it."

―――――――――――――――――――

[6] https://www.youtube.com/watch?v=EK3RaU6lPf4

Why is it so important to get VR right?

VR media, intermediate results, Presence and Agency

You might want to say: "VR is just another medium, so let's learn the rules and we are done." But that is not right. It is of the utmost importance to do VR the right way. And here is why.

VR media and intermediate results

First let us be clear about one thing. VR is not just headsets. But head mounted displays are right now (early 2017) seen as similar to VR. There are many more forms of virtual reality, like caves (where you wear simple stereo glasses), fulldomes (like in a planetarium) or something I am waiting for, digital multi user light field displays for which we won't need to wear glasses. I had the luck to personally do some experiments with static light field displays myself. For all of these different artificial reality creation techniques there are different rules for what is important.

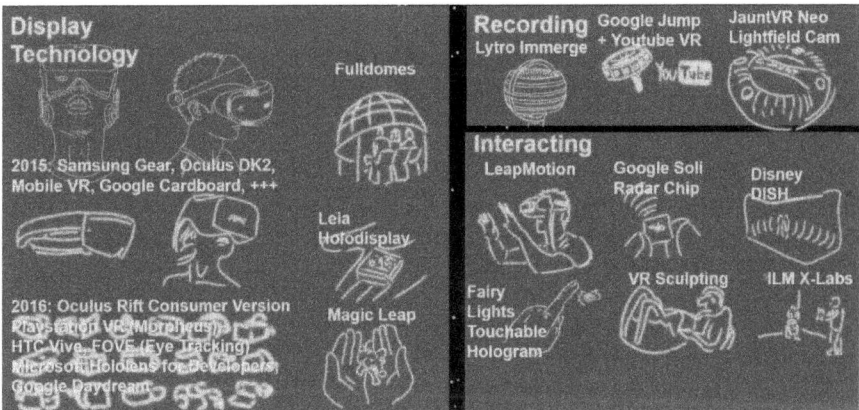

Figure 1: Virtual Reality is not just headsets

One consequence of this is: if you plan a VR movie that will be coming out some years in the future you must prepare for major adaptions of your work depending on the output medium it will run on. If you are wise you will organize your work in such a way that it can be used to "export" to various - today unknown - media. This means you as a director have to focus more on intermediate results as an important result layer of your work. This layer must become an integral part of your production pipeline. It has to be created and managed and it has to be documented very well because it might have to be stored and kept for years. In the future somebody might say: "O.K. let's create a light field dome version of this VR goggle experience." and you want it to be there in place to easily be used for this new revival. So, you as a director must not just create a VR movie. You must create a 3D meta experience from which you create one or more output media to be consumed by your audience. And for every output medium it is important to do it right. As technology is evolving very fast right now, and the same is true for VR standards, it doesn't make sense to teach you things for a specific headset or software. Rather we will focus on core principles for you to understand the craft of VR movie making. I hope this idea will keep this content valuable for a longer time than those "press-this-button-guides" that are outdated within less than a year.

Presence and Agency

In an ordinary movie you have some degree of immersion - more or less - depending on the size of the screen, the surrounding sound and maybe other stimuli like dbox motion seats. But you always have an anchor to the real world which is the static frame that stays in front of you. If you turn your head you see "the real world" and the screen stays where it is. Let's get back to VR headsets for now. If you have a VR headset strapped to your face and turn your head you expect the display to follow your head movement and show the correct part of the virtual world. You expect the spatial sound to relatively change position as well so that for you it seems the sound is emitted from the same places surrounding you. What is new with virtual reality is that you feed several technical output channels directly into the input of the audience's physical senses. You almost directly create interfaces to the nervous system, the ears and the sense of balance. The direct consequences are considerable. If done right the immersion is close to perfect and the person believes themself to actually be there. We call this "presence". If the audience expects to be able to manipulate the world because a hammer is lying just in front of them we call this "agency". If the audience can't grab the hammer the agency is broken. If the world behaves laggy the presence is broken. And even worse: if what you see doesn't match what your body feels it is an attack on your sense of balance. You get what we call "motion sickness" or "nausea". A colleague who had never experienced VR before tried a mobile VR ride from a major car brand that was badly produced. He got nausea and ever since has rejected VR as a bad thing in general. This shows that we as content producers have a great responsibility because with our VR productions we affect the perception of the whole VR industry. Motion sickness can be caused by many things, for example, bad latency - meaning that when you turn your head it takes too long for the headset or the software to get the right picture in front of you. There is a magical number - at about 90 frames per second (fps) - or roughly 11 milliseconds - where VR in a headset starts to feel as if you were really there. Please don't confuse the two kinds of fps. One is the fps that updates your image when you turn or move your head in VR. The other is the fps of a recorded video. It is perfectly O.K. to have a 360° video recorded and played back at 24 fps. But it is important that the update of the VR display when you turn your head happens way faster at 90+ fps, even if that means one video image lasts 3 fps. There is another thing that is important: parallax. This is a "displacement or difference in the apparent position of an object viewed along two (or more) different lines of sight"[7]. Let's conduct an experiment. Sit down on a chair and turn your head slowly from left to right. You will notice that objects closer to you move relatively to things that are in the background. Maybe you never consciously noticed this before but your brain always did. Our brain is a marvelous 3D real time computing unit. It determines the 3D structure of our surroundings by using exactly these slight differences in parallax. In an ordinary 360° movie - even if it is stereoscopic you don't have parallax. This means when you turn your head or try to look around an object with a VR headset you don't experience the slight parallax and your subconscious tells you it feels some kind

---

[7] Quote from https://en.wikipedia.org/wiki/Parallax

of odd. The stereoscopic effect in a 360° movie will also break if you turn your head sideways (roll) and place one eye above the other. You can avoid all of this by using a game engine and computing a real time image of the 3D scene for each eye 90 times per second. But this has other implications for performance depending on object and polygon count. There are other solutions we will discuss later.

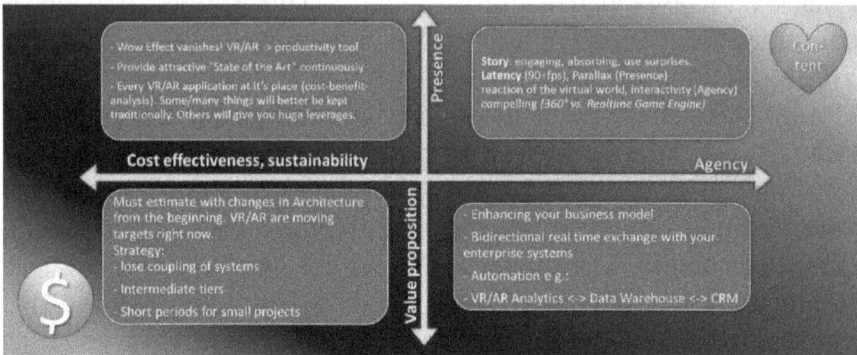

Figure 2: Balancing the Success Factors for great and profitable VR experiences

Conclusion

For now, it is enough to know: a good VR experience depends on many, many things. On the projection type (headset, fulldome, holographic or light field display, ...), the kind of projection (360° movie, monoscopic or stereoscopic vs. real time stereo render), the frame rate, the sound (roughly 50% of the immersion depends on the sound), haptical feedback, the agency you provide by the physically correct behavior of the world. And on many more things, some of them known today, some of them to be discovered in the next few years. It is mandatory to get things right because we build almost direct interfaces to our audience's nervous systems. It is so important to get a sufficient number of things right so that we create a good presence and a good agency for the audience. Then we have to add good, enjoyable content as well. Now I believe you are ready to face the truth. So, if you ask: "Is it harder to create a good VR movie than to create a good ordinary movie?", the answer is: "Yes, it is!" This means: more effort, more cost and more things to consider. And here is our moment of truth. The faint hearted should now stop reading and live a boring meaningless life - farewell. ...

... Are you still here? Good. Because now comes the more relevant question for you to ask. "Is it worth it?" The answer is: "Oh boy, yes, it is!" There are endless opportunities for us to boldly immerse our audience in worlds they have never experienced before. Cinematic VR done right is the closest safe thing to really being there. And who didn't always want to be right in a Hollywood movie when the action happens?

Part II

The cinematic VR Game - Your mission

"There's a difference between knowing the path and walking the path."

Morpheus to Neo in the Matrix

Preface I love 8-bit arcade games. The 1980s were the time I grew up and had my first C64 and a world of miracles opened to me. And I love the video arcades of those times. The movie TRON was the inspiration to me and millions of other people to get inside this fantastic computer world. And now VR is our portal to achieve this dream. So, I thought: "Let's make this in 8-bit 3D VR." Yeah, right.

O.K. We have a two-player game and you may want to accompany Player One to experience what he does right. You may also want to pay attention to Player Two who rather gets it wrong most of the time. Sorry, I didn't choose a girl for one of the players. But as I already had one player it would have been a difficult debate to give one of the roles to a girl and the other to a boy. So, girls, imagine two girls playing the game if you like that better. And now, let's play!

Player One and Player Two have inserted their coins already and are prompted with their mission:

"Your Mission: Make the greatest cinematic VR movie of all times and earn lots of money."

Figure 3: Your Mission for the cinematic VR Game

Level 1: Funding Your VR Movie and Thinking about ROI

"It was logical to cultivate multiple options."

Spock

Introduction

A VR production is more complex than an ordinary 2D or 3D movie production. Hence it is more expensive. It is as simple as that.

Sarah Hill, CEO of StoryUP states – as a ballpark figure – that a VR video costs at least three times that of a regular video (see her interview at http://vrroom.buzz/vr-news/trends/how-vr-will-change-content-marketing). Actually, she refers to 360° video production, not to other technological options like interactive experiences in game engines (which we will cover later in this book).

So, why should anyone ever finance a huge VR production?

21

No movie on a screen will immerse you like a VR experience. This also is as simple as that.

But investors often care more about ROI - their return on investment and about their profit. As we know very well there are ordinary movies that fail to return their investment, or those that earn their costs; and then there are the blockbusters. Of course, it would be nice to always create profit, but at the end of the day it is important to make sufficient profits as an average. An investor too afraid of losing his money with one single production might not be the right investor for you. There will be VR blockbusters and VR movie flops. There is no perfect way to predict the box office results.

This is not a detailed guide for how to raise money for a movie. Rather we focus on some aspects special to VR. There are some good guides out there on the web about getting your script accepted by a studio or about raising money for movies in general. I suggest that you utilize your trusted search engine to find some basic information.

With the huge opportunities of cinematic VR there also come risks. At this level, I will just put some thoughts together to help you find the financial resources for your VR movie production.

Small productions

Just go and make something awesome. Well, of course you will need money or at least resources, even for a small endeavor to create a good to awesome result. A crowdfunding campaign might help. My personal experience of trying to raise money from the crowd is: it is important to have already built up your fan base before entering the financing phase. This means you will have to create a lot of promo material upfront to gather your fans. Then crowdfunding is an excellent way to help to fund your project and increase your fan base as well as foster the relationship with your existing fans.

The Cinematic VR Formula

Large productions

We frequently see crowdfunding projects collecting millions of dollars. But making 50 to 80 million US dollars on Kickstarter will not work for all of us. So, you will have to go with one of the major studios and/or some wealthy progressive producers/investors. Here are some suggestions and propositions to inspire you for your negotiations.

Option A: Distribute risks - make a VR version and a movie theater version, plus some more stuff (360-degree approach).

Today's large movie projects anyway have some side formats and additional streams of revenue, ranging from merchandising, to licensing, to a game accompanying the movie and also a VR experience. Think about the great VR experience of "The Martian". As Spock put it: "It is logical to cultivate multiple options." And this is usual today. But what if you go for the VR experience to be the major attraction? Let's hear how Player One approaches his negotiation with the producer.

Figure 4: Player One approaches the producer for funding

Player One: "Dear producer. Let's create an amazing VR movie and earn lots of money."

The Cinematic VR Formula

Producer: "This is way too risky. Nobody did this before. I could lose all my money."
Player One: "Sure. The faint hearted will not follow this path to fame and fortune. But I have an idea how to mitigate the risk."
Producer: "Let me hear it. You have my full attention ... for another 30 seconds."
Player One smiles... for about ten seconds before continuing: "Well. We create an ordinary A movie and a VR version of it at the same time. The synergy effects will lead to only 1.5 times the cost but double your ROI chances. If the VR version doesn't work you still can make a good to huge profit with the cinema version."
Producer: "Hmmm... interesting idea. Now. You get another 10 seconds if you tell me where to get the additional funding from."
Player One smiles again: "Would this VR chance not be worth it to draw 10 percent from five of your other movie investments? Or let's say 5 percent from ten of your other movies?"
Producer nods his head and smiles: "Let's take some more time to talk about this interesting production..."
After a great dinner Player One receives the funding for his Hollywood blockbuster VR movie production and advances to the next level.

Option B: Full Risk on one Card

Meanwhile Player Two who couldn't get any known producers to talk to him negotiates with a Gangster Boss.

Player Two: "Thank you very much for your time, Sir."
Gangster Boss: "Don't worry son. You will pay me back, I am sure about that. So, now explain how this VR thing is going to make me lots of money."
Player Two: "Well, VR immerses the audience completely. So, it will be a much more powerful experience."
Gangster Boss: "That doesn't interest me. All I care for is the money it gets me. And it will do that, won't it?"
Player Two: "Ehm, of course Sir. Yes, yes."
Gangster Boss: "Good. All other results would really upset me. And you don't want to end up like Jimmy Hoffa, do you?"

The Cinematic VR Formula

Player Two: "Who? Eh ... What happened to him?"
Gangster Boss: "Oh. He was a union activist who became involved with organized crime. He simply disappeared in 1975. No one knows for sure what happened. But rumors are that somebody made him some cement shoes. I expected you to know that as it was part of the VR experience Chomp from the 1990s where Jimmy Hoffa was doing the wave underwater."
Player Two: "Uh oh. I understand perfectly, Sir."
Gangster Boss: "Great. So, you have one year to triple my money."
Player Two (shocked): "Triple?!"
Gangster Boss: "That won't be a problem, will it?"
Player Two: "Uh... Well. No. No problem. ... Sir."

Besides the strategies of Player One and Player Two here are some more hints that might help you with your project:

- Risk management: distribute risk over more than one VR production and non-VR productions.

- It has become quite common for larger, and increasingly for smaller productions, to use multiple revenue streams from the movie assets for different variations. Besides the VR movie and a standard cinema version this can be video games (VR- and non-VR-versions), novels extending the story, merchandising, licensing artwork, ... you name it.

- As VR-productions are more complex think twice about producing "breaking news"-like content that will lose attention in a short period of time. Instead think about producing long lasting plays like musicals or operas. This way you can go for long term revenue.

- Create hybrid results (e.g. an on-stage actor based theater performance combined with VR/MR elements). Activate your imagination to create something no one has ever seen before.

- As a consequence of rapid innovation you need to focus on intermediate results to be able to deliver to new output formats in the future to open up new revenue streams. And the consequence of this is: the known budget splitting ratios change for VR productions. Track and categorize your expenses to have forecast data for future VR productions. If you do this recording of data well it is possible that somebody might want to pay for this valuable information.

- Cultivate ROI from other sources: some examples - VR Analytics, advertisement, product placement, merchandising. I suggest you read the book "Virtual Reality Analytics" which I co-authored to dive deeper into this subject. In general, it is about analyzing user behavior during their consumption of the VR experience. An enhanced profiling of users is interesting to many companies using business intelligence data.

Conclusion

As VR is a relatively new medium and lessons have to be learned first before we achieve mastery there will be flops and losses. However there are good approaches to mitigate or distribute risk or to increase the pie. If you love your production idea you will surely find creative ways to persuade people to fund it.

Level 2: The Story

"People don't just watch a VR story; they feel it. ... Story combined with VR is a powerful tool for calm, joy, and empathy."

Sarah Hill, CEO and chief storyteller for StoryUP.[8]

VR itself is very immersive and powerful. You can excite people by putting them into a beautiful place. Or you can scare them to death by directly connecting to their brain and activating their

---

[8] http://vrroom.buzz/vr-news/trends/how-vr-will-change-content-marketing

fight or flight response.[9] And you can make them fall down by tricking their sense of balance (equilibrium). So, be aware of your power and always remember Stan Lee's words: "With great power comes great responsibility."

Yet the powerful immersive impression will fade the more people get used to VR and AR and the more common it is to use these technologies every day. When movies were young a train rapidly passing a station was enough to make people scream and freak out. Nobody screams today when watching a movie with a passing train. We are used to it.

So, what keeps people amazed in your VR productions is the story. It doesn't matter if the story is watched in a 3D cinema or told at a fireplace. What matters is what happens in the heads of the audience. This will remain when the excitement about the new medium slowly fades. So, a great story is more and more key to your success with VR movies. But what is a good story for VR?

What stories fit in VR?

In general: every good story fits in VR, but it has to be thoughtfully considered about how to present it to the audience. On the one hand VR gives us a bunch of new artistic opportunities. On the other hand, we can't just use all well-known successful movie maker tools because many of them work differently in VR or don't work at all. Two examples: 1. Cutting. Yes, you can cut in VR but you have to consider how this affects the audience's minds. There is not much cutting in reality and you don't jump from one place to another. Creating VR experiences with lots of rapid cutting and fast movement simply will make people sick. 2. Framing. Directors love to lead the audience's attention directly to a specific subject by only showing the subject surrounded by the frame of the screen. In VR, you can't avoid that the audience will turn their heads and watch something completely different. Damn. They will miss what you wanted to show them.

---

[9] https://en.wikipedia.org/wiki/Fight-or-flight_response

So, the rules change with VR. This is why traditional movies will remain and VR will enrich our world of media experiences. Yet there is a category we can learn a lot from: classic theater. VR is similar to theater in many ways with the additional bonus that you can create and prerecord magnificent scenery. Think about not only seeing a play of the Titanic on stage while you sit in your chair but be at the captain's table when you crash into that iceberg. We will get to those aspects in a later chapter. For now, it is important to remember: every good story fits in VR, but it may need some special ideas for how to tell this story - or better, how to enable people to experience the story. If you think you have encountered a story that definitely doesn't fit in VR please write to me. I would love to think about how we can make it work in VR.

Figure 5: Bestselling stories usually will work in movies as well as in VR

Storytelling vs. World Building

In 2015 at FMX in Stuttgart (I really recommend FMX) the big subject was storytelling in VR. In 2016 at FMX the subject evolved. The main message was: it's not about telling a story but about building worlds where the audience can explore and experience the story. This allows the free will of the audience to vary their experience. So, we don't talk about just telling a linear story anymore. Rather more it's about building a story network with branches. You might say: "This would be far more complex and need more time and effort." Yes, you are right. But we know that from the past. When I was young in the 1980s we had fantasy role playing books with small chapters ending with something like: "Do you want to attack the troll with your blue glowing blade? Then read on at chapter 123. If you decide to escape through the green door continue at chapter 234." So, yes. It needs more work to create a good story for VR. But it can be handled and is worth the effort. Here we see the strong influence of video games and we can learn from that. The more interactive a VR movie is, the more intense is the engagement of the audience, and the more challenging is the technical creation of such a piece. In fact, there will come a break-even point where it isn't feasible anymore to create a story network. Rather you will need to turn your world into a simulation like in a game where NPCs (non-player-characters) strive for certain goals and the story unfolds automatically. There is always a tradeoff between both concepts - story network and simulation.

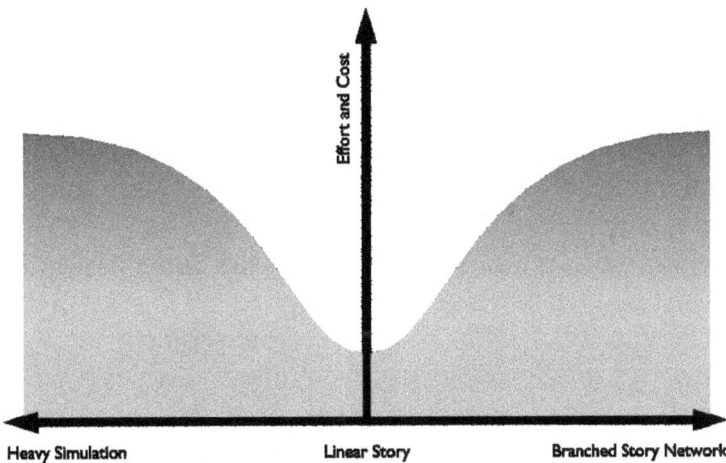

Figure 6: Simulation building effort vs. story network complexity

I expect to see many hybrid approaches incorporating some part of simulation working together with some part of story network. It is not that far away from those great text adventures back in the

1980s when we played Zork on our C64s, so it can be handled. And we see more and more authoring tools for such kind of content coming to the market to ease the creation of condition-based story telling. One of the first was the software Panotour from kolor.com (now owned by GoPro, creators of action cams often used as 360° rigs).

Let's see how Player One and Player Two handle this level to get the perfect story for their VR movie.

Player One's chat with a best-selling author

Player One: Thank you for your time. It is an honor that you share your experience as a best-selling author with me.
Best-selling author: You are welcome. What can I do for you?
Player One: I need a great story that fits in Virtual Reality to create the greatest VR movie of all time and earns lots of money.
Best-selling author: That is specific. Good. I think I can tell you something about a good story which is always is a lot of work.
Player One: Please, go on.
Best-selling author: First - if you are the author - it has to come from your heart. It must be something that relates to you and your life. Something that is awfully important to you. Your mission on the planet. At least your mission at the moment. Next, you just go and write it. Don't make it perfect yet. Maybe you will rewrite parts of it. But just let the magic flow. Then bring in some other people.
Player One: Other people?
Best-selling author: Yes. You need an editor. Someone who loves the subject you wrote about. When I wrote my first sci-fi novel I hired a professional editor who also wrote sci-fi stories. I learned a lot from her. She taught me to keep my pov - my point of view. And she taught me to run certain tests with my story. To go into every character of a scene and be him, then ask myself: would he really do this? She tore some scenes completely apart. And we had some fine battles about things that were important to me that she didn't think fit in the story. And in the end, it was a great story.
Player One: This was the first person. You mentioned people.

The Cinematic VR Formula

Best-selling author: Oh yes. Later I brought in a proofreader to fix my broken sentences and watch that my commas are in the right place. Also, as it was a real book on real paper I brought in a typesetter. Then I published it with my own publishing business that I had founded for that.

Player One: You as a best-selling author didn't get a publisher?

Best-selling author: Not at the beginning. I researched over 5,000 publishers, wrote to many of them but they are all so busy since everybody wants to publish their stuff. So, I thought I could wait forever or I could just do it myself. And I did. It wasn't that hard. And later when my books were successful suddenly publishers showed up. Today I choose whether to publish a story myself or whether to use the marketing force of a major label and go with them.

Player One: Wooooow!

Best-selling author: Yes. But we are here to talk about a good story, aren't we?

Player One: Oh yes, of course.

Best-selling author: Well I believe that is my part. You know what I did from the first moment on? I imagined every scene in my book like a Hollywood action movie. And it worked. So, when people read it they see this action movie in their head. And of course - as I said in the beginning - you need to have an important and great story with lots of emotion and some fun.

Player One: Wow. Thanks. That was a good tip having the movie in your head. Yes, I read some of your books. It is true. I feel I'm in the midst of a movie.

Best-selling author: Nice to hear that.

Player One: And then comes the conversion to VR. You know, if you have an action scene with lots of cuts and camera movement you can't do that in VR as people would get confused and simply vomit. So, there needs to be an adaption.

Best-selling author: Ah. I see. Like an adaption from novel to screenplay.

Player One: Yes, yes. I need to take a great story and create some sort of VR-play for it. Oh - and as we decided to also produce an ordinary 3D movie for cinemas we also need a screenplay. Wow. This is going to be more work than I thought. And where do I get this story from?

Best-selling author: Maybe I could help. You know, some of my novels have been converted to Hollywood blockbusters. But some are still waiting for this honor. And as my first novel GameW0rldz was a Virtual Reality Story and an AI Robot story I have some expertise. I even conducted my own neural network programming experiments. You don't write a bestseller without doing some research, you know.

Player One: And you want to offer me that story to get a VR production?

Best-selling author: Actually no. It would be a good choice but we could go even further.

Player One: Further?

Best-selling author: I wrote a sequel to GameW0rldz. It is called 3futurez. It is about the future of humanity facing artificial intelligence and the technological singularity. It has everything to make a great movie. And there are also some alien races discovered as well. The world faces great opportunities and enormous threats. And as it is intended to be a Hollywood story it includes a love story as well that might destroy or save the Earth.

Player One: Wow. That sounds weird.

Best-selling author: And I have planned a VR-play for some time in the form of a holodeck musical.

Player One: You are kidding, aren't you?

Best-selling author: Young man, did you really prepare for this conversation? You seem to be somewhat uninformed. I have given talks about this for years now.

Player One: Oh, sorry sir. (mumbles to himself: damn, I should have checked his website more closely). We had lots of time pressure and I wasn't able to do a complete background check.

Best-selling author: Relax, rookie. I can imagine a great theater version of 3futurez with or without music. Maybe better without - so it is a pure action movie. And the musical version which only is available in Virtual Reality.

Player One: This would cause people to view it twice. Once on the screen and once in VR. It would help sales to keep them distinct.

Best-selling author: And yet we can reuse a lot of the work, recordings and assets for both parts.

Player One: That sounds really great. But what would you want for that bestseller story?

Best-selling author: Just a small fee plus a percentage of the revenue.

Player One: I think we should have a talk with the producer tomorrow.

Best-selling author: Very well.

Player Two's chat

Player Two: Thanks for joining this chat with me. So, you can create for me a great story as a ghostwriter for five bucks, right?

Guy from fiverr[10]: Very true sir. I can makes best story of world.

Player Two: You know our budget is a bit restricted. We are planning a VR movie production and it is insanely expensive so we need to save money somewhere. I thought we could begin with the story as all stories seem the same to me.

Guy from fiverr: I can make best story, sir.

Player Two: Yes. What would you put in it?

Guy from fiverr: What you need sir?

Player Two: My ... my customer wants to have a powerful gangster boss being the hero, robbing the bank, falling in love with a top model and saving the world so he is elected to President of the United States. Would people like that?

Guy from fiverr: I can do that sir. But with so many things in it it gets a longer story. This would mean I need 5 times as much. So, 25 bucks.

Player Two: Are you crazy? You are ruining me. No way.

Guy from fiverr: O.K. 15 bucks then?

Player Two: Deal.

Guy from fiverr: You will have your story until tuesday.

Player Two: And it will be of the best-selling quality, won't it?

---

[10] www.fiverr.com is an interesting platform for affordable services/crowd sourcing I have already tried myself with very mixed results. To be clear – there were great people offering high quality services – but there were also the others...

Guy from fiverr: Of course sir. Me work always is rated best. See? People give me 5 stars.

Player Two: Oh - and it has to fit perfectly in VR.

Guy from fiverr: What is VR?

Player Two: Damn, just send me the script by Tuesday.

Guy from fiverr: Have nice day, Sir. You will not be dessapointat.

Conclusion

- Most great stories fit in VR. It just has to be considered how to present them to the audience.
- As VR is a very powerful medium, along with that comes a great responsibility for you as cinematic VR creative.
- If your story is bad, go back and improve it or choose a great story. I have already recommended the book: "The Writer's Journey"[11] by Christopher Vogler. Also check out James N.Frey's book: "How to Write a Damn Good Novel"[12]
- VR won't replace movies just as movies haven't replaced radio or theater. They will enrich our world of experiences.
- We can learn a lot from theater for cinematic VR as both share many aspects.
- A VR storyteller's work is rather to create a story network, or maybe a simulation. Tradeoffs between both lead the way as to when to use which technique and where to mix both.
- You don't just tell a story but you build a world in which your story can be experienced and felt by the audience.

Level 3: What is your screen?

"My God, It's Full of Stars!"

David Bowman in the movie:
"2001: A Space Odyssey" from 1968.

---

[11] https://www.amazon.de/Writers-Journey-Mythic-Structure/dp/193290736X/

[12] https://www.amazon.de/Write-Damn-Novel-Step-Step/dp/0312010443/

Now you have a great story that is VR ready. Brilliant. So, let's move on to level 3 where we will meditate about what your screen is. And in level 4 we will continue our meditation thinking about many technological aspects based on our results of level 3.

Now close your eyes... wait! Are you still there? I forgot. You won't be able to read with closed eyes unless you are from Krypton. So, please close only your virtual eyes and relax. Take a deep breath. Empty your mind. Free your spirit until you can clearly hear the god of VR who will throw a bunch of questions at you. Your relaxed mind will easily build a beautiful construct from them and give the answers for your production... or you might completely panic. But don't worry. There is a solution for every direction you are heading in - even if you choose multiple directions at once. And you are not alone. Player One and Player Two are with you as well.

Here we go. Can you three hear the VR God's voice speaking to you?

1. Where and how will the audience experience your VR movie?
2. In what social context will they experience it?
3. How long will it be?
4. What senses are addressed?
5. What does the audience of your target platform expect and how does that influence your type of content?
6. What future distribution and presentation formats might we think of?

Are you confused? Good! Muhahaha. Ehm. Sorry. Now let's bring some light into the darkness. I will repeat my questions and get into more detail for each one. Ready? O.K. Round two.

1. Where and how will the audience experience your VR movie?

People might experience your VR movie on their couch at home with a mobile (smartphone based) headset. Or they might do it at a dedicated location (out of home entertainment/location based entertainment LBE/5D). But all of these options need one thing: a "screen" onto which the experience is projected using various methods. Unless we talk about future distribution formats at question 6 we will always have a screen. Will it be a head mounted display (VR headset?). This means two distinct images are computed about 90 times per second (or more frequently) to show you a stereoscopic, probably slightly tilted, section of the complete world which is 360°x180°. Do you project into a digital fulldome (which is the upper half of a sphere like in planetariums)? There are several strategies for how to project onto that fulldome ranging from using a mirror ball and having just one or two projectors up to using multiple projectors and dealing with overlapping problems. We can't dive deeper here, because this would go way beyond our scope. The next question: is it monoscopic or stereoscopic (3D)?

You also could refit a classic 3D cinema. Add a screen at the walls right and left to the audience, one to the back and one behind. Also, project to those walls. Use rounded corners to avoid them being seen. At Disney they constructed such an environment which they call the DISH - Digital Immersive SHowroom. The only difference? They project onto the floor instead of the ceiling. But think of it as just turning this upside down to refit your 3D cinema. Yes. Projector technology is expensive. Especially if you want to project to a flat screen including rounded corners and overlapping or perfectly fitting seams. But: you can re-use your cinema premises. Your ordinary 3D glasses still work. So, besides a one-time investment the operating costs should be rather limited. And you get a full blown immersive 3D cinema.

It quickly becomes clear that we might have to adopt our source material to the projection method. We can't rely on just converting one format to another due to possible quality loss or stitching errors, especially when it comes to 3D where you need depth information for accurate stitching results. It is an even greater difference if you recalculate your stereo view live for a VR headset.

From the developments we have seen so far, more and more software takes away the pain from the creatives and automates tasks like creating a pair of stereo VR spheres. When I started with VR projection at the end of 2014 I created my own render solution which was: calculate one or only some pixel columns of an equirectangular sphere, turn the camera and repeat that until you have covered all 360°. Then stitch each pixel column together. And voila - your stereo sphere is ready and working. Today this functionality is a standard ability of your 3D software, or you should be able to get a plugin for it. Anyway, it is a good idea to understand the basics and do some experiments for yourself. This will ease the process of problem analysis when things go wrong in your production - and as the technology is complex there will indeed be things that go wrong. Ask Murphy.

2. In what social context will they experience it?

The social context also depends on your projection method. If you are watching something in a fulldome you can see the surrounding audience. It is a social experience. This also means each person sees the result from the same camera position which locks the viewer position not offering parallax when strafing with the head. Your brain notices this somewhat artificial feeling. For smaller size fulldomes an alternative technology might be interesting. There is a solution called CastAR which uses two mini projectors in lightweight polarized glasses that allows multi user experiences. (Unfortunately CastAR closed its gates in Summer 2017[13]) This also calculates individual images for each viewer, but it is probably limited to a small number of people due to the power of the mini projectors. If you wear a VR headset instead you are completely immersed in it and typically all of your surroundings are blocked out, so, you won't see the people in the room with you. There are companies trying to re-incorporate those social elements by re-transferring those people back into

---

[13] https://www.polygon.com/2017/6/26/15877804/castar-shut-down

your VR environment. As the technology evolves rapidly we will have to wait to see which widely accepted standards develop.

3. How long will it be?

The duration of your play depends on many factors. If you are in a theme park the length might be restricted by the length of the accompanying ride like a virtual reality coaster ride. (www.vrcoaster.de) Or you want to put some hundreds or some thousands of people through each day so it is only some minutes long. It also might be a 90-minute experience. Play time increases from year to year. It also depends on the projection method again. I can hardly imagine strapping a brick onto my face for two hours. But I can imagine wearing lightweight cinema 3D glasses for that period of time. This is why we have to collect our experiences and learn from what works.

4. What senses are addressed?

This also depends on your delivery environment. You always have visual and audio output. Spatial sound (that comes from the right directions and is reflected properly from surrounding surfaces) is responsible for about 50% of the quality of the immersive experience. Surprisingly sound design doesn't usually get 50% of the movie budget. Depending on the installation other senses might be added like: wind, temperature, movement, smell. An installation like a shower cabin I visited in Spain was interesting as it added the heat of the sun and the smell of pine trees to a location where I visited a luxury estate in the Mediterranean. This truly enhanced the immersion. Other technologies are in development, for example in-ear manipulation of your sense of balance using special headphones. This especially makes sense if you are trying to avoid motion sickness and/or want to simulate motion (Read the Article: "Samsung developing headphones to stimulate ear nerves"[14]) . However, we may see some new

---

[14] http://www.dailymail.co.uk/sciencetech/article-3494981/Samsung-developing-headphones-make-feel-like-moving-Entrim-4D-stimulates-ear-nerves-make-VR-real.html

developments, surprises and failures in the future. Also think about: what works for large audiences? And: is everything that can be done wise to do, to increase the immersion as far as we can? You sure don't want a cinema full of people getting motion sick at the same time because of your production (or because somebody hacked your balance manipulator system).

As VR directly connects to our senses it is important to be involved in the distribution planning. Because: what works well in an entertainment location including movement might work out to be fatal if bluntly ported to a mobile download version harming people in their homes. So, always make clear that with VR the creative people need to be involved in all output channels as they might need adaptions to avoid negative perception of the studio.

5. What does the audience of your target platform expect and how does that influence your type of content?

People visiting a theater or musical to enjoy an immersive artistic experience might have a different expectation regarding your play from the hardcore gamer who is mostly playing first person horror shooters using the steam gaming platform. It is always good to have a look at: what are the typical customers used to when it comes to pricing, onboarding, offboarding, complexity of installation, tutorials interwoven into your experience, the possibility of sharing precious moments and talking about it (chats, comments, in-game-re-streaming...). Here it is wise to dig into the numbers. What content do people of this platform like? How much competition is there? How do your results have to be customized to that platform for maximum commercial success?

6. What future distribution and presentation formats might we think of?

Am I the VR God or am I not? Yes, I am. And here comes my favorite genre: science fiction... or so I thought a while ago. Let's have a closer look. The goal is the holodeck or some kind of perfect VR illusion like in the matrix to enslave... er ... to let you enjoy the wonders of VR and make your dreams come true. No seriously. I believe it is important that you have strong mental roots in the real world to create a valuable multiverse of virtual realities. Otherwise you would use VR as an escape from the real world which is not good at all because many would abandon the real world instead of helping to improve it.

But let's get back to technology. All things we are discussing now are in an early prototyping stage. But none of it is science fiction any longer. Nor does it need any quantum leap to get to the next technology stage. All we need is some time, the linear progress of iterative improvements and Moore's law. So, with all of this the question isn't, will it come, but when will it be affordable for the masses? Let's start with Mixed Reality. MR is here already. The Microsoft HoloLens is a great piece of technology that puts artificial 3D graphics in our world interactively. The first model has some limitations but give it time and let's wait to see what others bring to the market like Meta, MagicLeap (Lightfield technology) or Apple. Prepare yourself for creating augmented movies that mix computer graphics with our surrounding reality.

Next example: light field displays. This is the third immersive wave sometimes called USEMIR: Ubiquitous SEnsory MIxed Reality. This is when we take our glasses off and the magic remains. The author of this book had the honor of conducting some experiments with real light field displays on an analog basis. Analog because the necessary resolution to put a complete render image behind 250,000 lenses is insane at about 18,000 dpi. But there are already prototypes of OLED displays capable of such an insane resolution. So, let's give it some time. Meanwhile the author of this book has developed a concept of how to create real time multi user digital light field displays. Again - only linear progress is necessary. But that is another story.

We can build immersive light fields in several variations. As walls, as rounded cubes or as domes. They are candidates for optically completely immersive environments - or holodecks as we know them from Star Trek. They are a great stage for a lot of immersive content and have some magical tricks. If you combine them with eye tracking you can save render time by just rendering the appropriate section of the image which is far less than 360°x180°.

The Cinematic VR Formula

And it gives you the opportunity to create different environments for different people staring at the same screen. He sees an ad for beer while she views a romantic novel and the guy next to them safely checks his bank account. All in public space. USEMIR will be way more phantastic than all of you Earthlings imagine right now. Oh. An alternative to such a light field display would be a laser projection directly onto your retina. Let's see which tech will win the battle. But it doesn't matter for you as content creator.

And the hologram floating in mid-air like Princess Leia is also here already. A group presented their work with a multi laser installation that heats the air until it converts to a plasma that glows. Fortunately, they use femtosecond lasers which protects your skin from being burned when you touch it. They also developed a way that the hologram interactively changes. Besides other things they built an aerial checkbox. Find their press kit here[15]. and their impressive video here[16].

We can expect virtual and mixed worlds to merge. It will be very common for us to have this 3dimensional multi reality on top of our world. I discovered a nice simple example of this blending approach on VVROOM[17].

As I said - none of this is science fiction any more. But as I love it so much here comes some real sci-fi.

Let's imagine our future even further. What if we won't need any display devices? What if we could directly beam VR and MR into our senses or our brain. Would you like that? Many (but not all) people would reject a technology that requires surgery. But if it was non-invasive? If you could manipulate your visual nerve with electromagnetic waves? The future will show if those things await humans around the corner. Now Earthlings this was some heavy

---

[15] http://digitalnature.slis.tsukuba.ac.jp/2015/06/fairy-lights-in-femtoseconds/

[16] https://youtu.be/AoWi10YVmfE

[17] http://www.vrroom.buzz/vr-news/products/hololens-vive-dev-creates-shared-reality

stuff. All three of you have passed this level. Now take a break in a virtual meditation or something. You earned it. After relaxing prepare for the next level where you will go deep down to some technology fundamentals.

Conclusion

There are many aspects to consider when planning a VR movie. We have covered some aspects to think about before starting. Read many news articles and keep your mind open for future possibilities here so you will always have new ideas with which you can surprise your audience.

Level 4: The realm of technology: render methods, their implications and emerging standard formats

"I do not think it possible to go further in the rendering of form."

Edgar Degas, French Painter 1834-1917

With level 3 mastered let's continue our meditation in level 4 and think more deeply about technology. It is time to start building your production pipeline. And time to make some decisions.

We stand at the gates of the realm of technology. Player One and Player Two will join you, each of you riding your own magic carpet slowly gliding above the tech landscape while you pick the components of your production pipeline. The gates open. Sit down and fasten your carpet-belt.

We spoke a lot about different projection techniques. Now we will leave this to one side and shift our focus to head mounted displays or in short: VR goggles. Let's think about how the images are created during viewing time and put into the headsets of the audience. This task is called rendering.

Down there you can see the three rivers of rendering. The river of pre-rendering, the river of realtime 3d and in the middle the river of hybrid rendering. Each of them follows separate rules and leads to different results. I will explain and you must choose wisely.

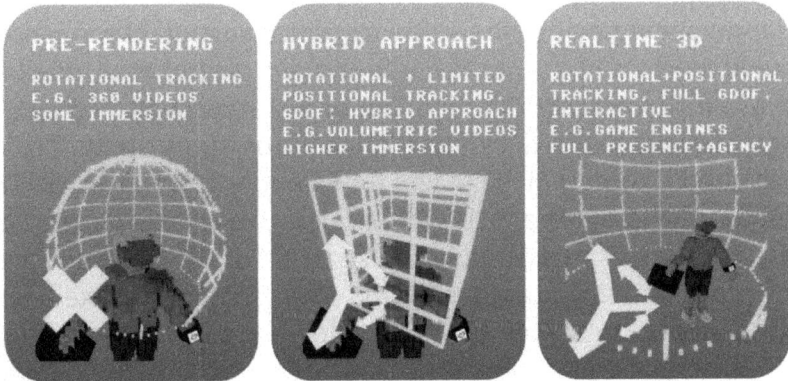

Figure 7: Different projection methods for VR have many technical implications

Pre-rendering

The first method is to record and stitch live action or to digitally create a scene and render the results onto a surrounding object like a 6-sided cube you are in or an equirectangular sphere which is a sphere with 360°x180° projected on a flat image with an aspect ratio of 2:1 like 8000x4000 pixels. If you want stereoscopy you have to render two of those spheres - one for each eye. There are many VR video players supporting this format where one eye is placed over the other eye. It is called Over-Under format. In our example this would produce an ordinary video file with 8000x8000 pixels. The sound, frame rate and other gimmicks like reference frames are determined by the video format and codec itself. One platform that accepts such videos is YouTube with its 360° format or YouTube VR for stereoscopic 360° videos. You have to check the specific platform you are using as to whether or not you have to inject special encodings to the video so that the platform recognizes it as VR video. Usually software is provided by the platform vendor to achieve this.

The Cinematic VR Formula

Let's say you uploaded your video to YouTubeVR. After processing by YouTube you can watch it with VR goggles like a Google Cardboard. You see your immersive movie in impressive 3D VR. But what happens here? Your video is just a projection onto two spheres surrounding you. It is a flat screen. With your head movement you tell the software which section of the screen it should select and put on the left or right part of your display. Your brain then creates the illusion of a stereoscopic sensation. Voila. As this is just a flat movie some restrictions apply. Try to look around an object close to you for example. It won't work. Try to tilt your head sideways. It will break the stereoscopic illusion because the two spheres have the sections of the different eyes aligned horizontally, not vertically. The content is fixed and without intelligence. You just have colors on two screens. If you can live with those restrictions you are fine with this render method. This also means there are consequences for analytical processing of your movie while people are watching. In a game engine you can do a Raycast to query which objects were in the line of sight. Here you can't. You just have rotation information from your audience. The translation to meaning has to occur separately. More information on this subject can be found in the book: Virtual Reality Analytics.

The advantage of this simple projection format is that you can create the visually perfect Hollywood quality experience. Playback is cheap and can be easily done with widely available mobile smartphone headsets. And it is clear what the maximum necessary resolution will be. You look surprised. It is 21600x10800x2 pixels of course. You ask why? Well, I suggest you check the facts yourself but if they are all correct here is why. In a talk at FMX 2015 the speaker said the maximum resolution of the fovea is 60 pixels per degree. 60x360=21600 and 60x180=10800. Times two because you want it in stereoscopy, right? So, no VR video needs higher resolution. Unless of course... Well, unless we increase our resolution by genetic engineering or something in the future. Or unless it is a good idea to store more information like it is done in the recording of light field information where you have sub pixel based information on color, distance and orientation. We share some thoughts about that later in this chapter when looking at the hybrid approaches. O.K. Let's say you have your max resolution chosen. I tried 8000x4000 which is roughly 8K. It gives you good detail in general but already demands a good bandwidth and computing power when using YouTube VR (remember, stereoscopy doubles the resolution to 8000x8000). Anyway the equirectangular format wastes a lot of information when it gets closer to the poles. In the top and bottom rows you waste the entire resolution representing one pixel. There are other projection techniques (like cubemaps) or other formats that have been developed that deal more efficiently with storage space. As development is fast here you should regularly check, what is the state of the art.

Realtime 3D

Now hang on and let's leave the river of pre-rendering. We are heading to the river of realtime 3D. There it is at the horizon. Now pull this fringe of the carpet. Waaaaiiit - not that strong. Wooosh. We are here already. Good God. It was wise that you fastened your carpet-belt. Now take a breath and look at the river of realtime 3D.

We create realtime VR usually by using a game engine or by some frameworks like WebVR/ThreeJS. Remember the good old days when we used VRML back in the 1990s. This Virtual Reality Modeling Language was a complete approach which included everything you wanted. Programmability in Java or Javascript, animation, spatial sound, hyperlinks to other VR worlds. Its successor X3D never became that popular for some reason. What technical solutions I see today early 2017 are poorer compared to back then because they lack this completeness and openness. Instead of one standard language you have many choices but most of them come with restrictions like no external links because otherwise people won't subscribe to our platform and won't pay for it. It is not the same spirit as in the 1990s where we wanted to create the free and open metaverse. But time will show if for example WebVR is able to regain this open environment again.

The Cinematic VR Formula

We started talking about game engines. Some game engines can also create output for WebGL which is OpenGL in your browser and which is also used as a basis for WebVR. So, maybe we will get to feature-richer and more open applications like back in the late 1990s that way. Right now, there are some major game engines heavily supporting virtual (and augmented) reality. First: Unity3D, the Unreal Engine and the Cryengine from Crytek. Also, Crytek's Film Engine which they bought for cinematic VR which comes from another technological base. All of them offer VR support for certain headsets by integration of plugins or prefabs from those vendors. Headsets with different technical abilities mean different options for programming them. Thus it is wise to use some kind of abstraction layer to be flexible with your output options. But let's have a look at what those game engines do. Game engines have a game logic, the 3D models of the whole scene including their animation data and usually some physics simulation. Every frame of the scene is then calculated - twice for VR, with the goal of achieving 90 frames per second at least which is roughly 11 milliseconds. That is a tough job. It is why graphics cards manufacturers like Nvidia or AMD are pushing the bounds lately and use many technological tricks to get an optimal VR performance. By the way it isn't done with image rendering. NVidia for example brought in the idea to use the raytracer (usually used for image calculation) to calculate realistic spatial sound considering reflections from your 3D surroundings. Technology advances are quite fast here and allow us to create realtime 3D today, unthinkable some years ago. Yet it has limitations as it can't be scaled endlessly. If it works well with let's say 10 simulated characters with 30,000 polygons each you can maybe do this with 20 or 50 characters as well but not with thousands. The same for heavy volumetric particle effects. The more 3D complexity you throw at it the slower it gets. There are approaches to deal with that like tesselation (also known under other names) which reduces the subdividing of objects to the necessary screen resolution but you will reach performance limits. And not everybody has a high end graphics card at hand. The charm of game engines is that you create your VR experience and then just deploy it onto many platforms ranging from high end PCs to low end mobile VR which usually have way weaker graphics power. And you don't want to drain a mobile user's batteries within a quarter of an hour. On the one hand you should restrict the complexity of your scene for real time but on the other hand you can cheat a bit by using pre-rendered VR movies to enhance your scene. For example: do the action close to the viewer in realtime 3D. For everything further away than X meters use a pre-rendered equirectangular projection. From a certain distance you can't distinguish the stereoscopic effect with your eyes. This means for things far enough away a monoscopic single pre-rendered sphere is sufficient. The distance I have heard about varies from source to source. This may be due to the resolution of today's VR headsets. But again, we can consult our fovea resolution of 60 pixels per degree. You won't need a differentiation if this pixel stays the same. So, we can use the rule of three (intercept theorem) to calculate at what distance we don't need stereoscopy any more.

The advantage of realtime 3D is that you have a real parallax when you look around an object as well as when you tilt your head. Looking at the development of the graphics cards industry producing better and better GPUs (graphical processing units) realtime 3D might be the choice in the future. Besides this you can create your VR experience completely interactively which is important for what we call "agency" in VR.

Hybrid rendering

Wouldn't it be great if we could combine the advantages of realtime 3D (parallax) and pre-rendered Hollywood quality in a hybrid approach? Yes, it is on the market already. Now pull that fringe more softly and let's advance to the river of hybrid rendering. Wooosh. That was way better than the last time. Now look down at this magnificent river.

I tried the PresenZ Experience of Nozon at FMX in 2015. It was amazing. I experienced a movie as well as a still image with full pre-rendered parallax. The awesome thing was: even the still image appeared to me as a real space I was in as I could tilt my head and look around objects. Apart from some issues of the early days of VR like the screendoor effect it was a perfect presence experience. I was able to enjoy the 6 degrees of freedom within the limits of a cube of one cubic meter which usually is enough for people sitting in a chair. At FMX 2016 I spoke to Tristan again, one of the founders of Nozon, who told me they enlarged their precomputed space. So, you can decide as a customer that you want a Hollywood quality VR movie in which you can walk around at room scale. Wow! Nozon was acquired by Starbreeze. We shall see what comes out of this. But let's now spend some thoughts on the technology behind it keeping in mind that there are some patents involved.

Existing and emerging formats and the chance for standardization

We cannot look at every approach of projection and rendering but I want to give some examples for your general understanding.

The Gordon's Arcade VR Prerender hack: First this is more a raw concept than a working 3D VR format, but maybe it, or some parts of it, could help in creating a pre-rendered VR format that can be stored cheaply. I want to stretch your brain muscles with this approach. It is well described in <u>my post to blenderartists.org which I quote here.</u>[18]

--- 8< ------------------------------------

I wonder if this kind of approach (or call it hack) might work to get parallax to VR rendered scenes even if I tilt my head. I have the hope that some of you have some answers to my questions below - as my idea if put to work would improve our VR viewing experience significantly.

---

[18] https://blenderartists.org/forum/showthread.php?414516-Flexible-Virtual-Reality-parallax-with-Blender-Tetrahedron-Multi-Camera-VR-View-Hack&p=3143867#post3143867

The Cinematic VR Formula

My thoughts are based on the fact that you get sufficient results with light field data if you don't use a complete array of your scene but only the frame outside plus an X inside the frame to interpolate the missing positions.

Now to my approach: imagine if we had not only the color information of our equirectangular scene in mono or stereo but also depth information from four different camera positions placed at the spikes of a tetrahedron: right, left, top, rear - each equirectangular (ER). In an ordinary ER VR scene we have two images e.g. over-under. Now we could (ab)use one of the images to store the depth information in of each of the four cameras in each channel: Red, Green, Blue, Alpha - voila - 4 ER images. Plus the other color image for the "texture" of the depth maps.

Now my questions as I am no math expert.

1. Would it work (or under what circumstances would it work) to "interpolate" an arbitrary viewer position within the tetrahedron to get the most accurate depth information from the 4 depth maps? I assume (as in my example) it gets problematic if I have objects within the tetrahedron itself (or if they are too close). Also I expect problems with parts of the geometry that are not visible from the outer camera positions but would be visible from positions in between.

2. Of course - related to the first point - it is also problematic to have parts of the ER texture missing (or at the wrong coordinates) depending on your viewpoint. Any suggestions for how to increase the texture information from more angles without using more image space?

3. As OpenEXR format seems to also store Z information would there be other ways or formats to achieve the goal of calculating depth information and putting textures on them on the fly in real time (using a game engine), or maybe with the OpenEXR MultiLayer format (without the file size exploding)? Are there any other formats that should be capable of this (Alembic, thinking about Google Spotlight stories)?

4.	I have met Tristan from Nozon.com twice. With PresenZ[19] they offer parallax VR experiences by taking your 3D data and rendering them into a magic format that also provides parallax in VR stills and videos. You should definitely check out their demo e.g. from Steam[20]. Nozon was acquired by Starbreeze last year[21]. Do you know whether their approach is similar to my idea or if it works completely differently?

Here are some image references:
a) The VR Sphere[22] (equirectangular stereo - will produce a photosphere view in a browser)

b)	2017-01-21a.VR_DepthmapCamTetrahedron.jpg

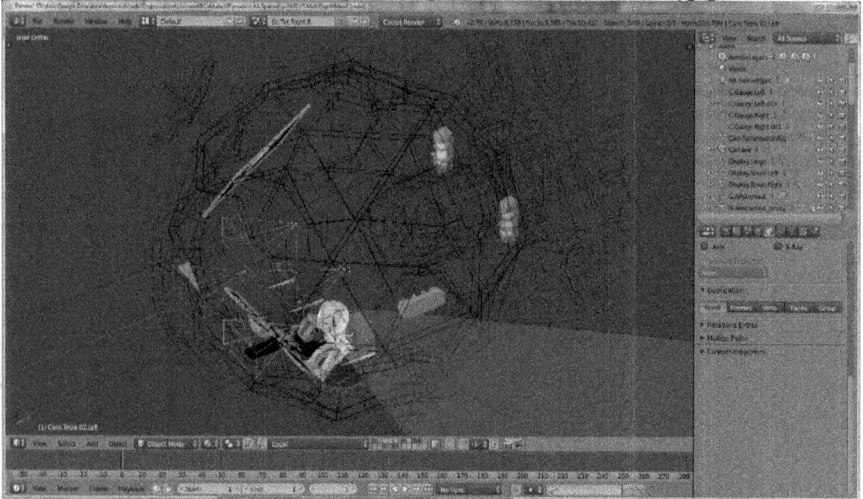

Figure 8: 3D Model of Alex' Space Ship in wireframe mode

[19] http://nozon.com/presenz

[20] http://store.steampowered.com/app/404020/

[21] https://uploadvr.com/starbreeze-acquires-nozon/

[22] http://vrais.io/?Kvvz6n

The Cinematic VR Formula

c)   2017-01-21b.VR_DepthmapRendering.jpg

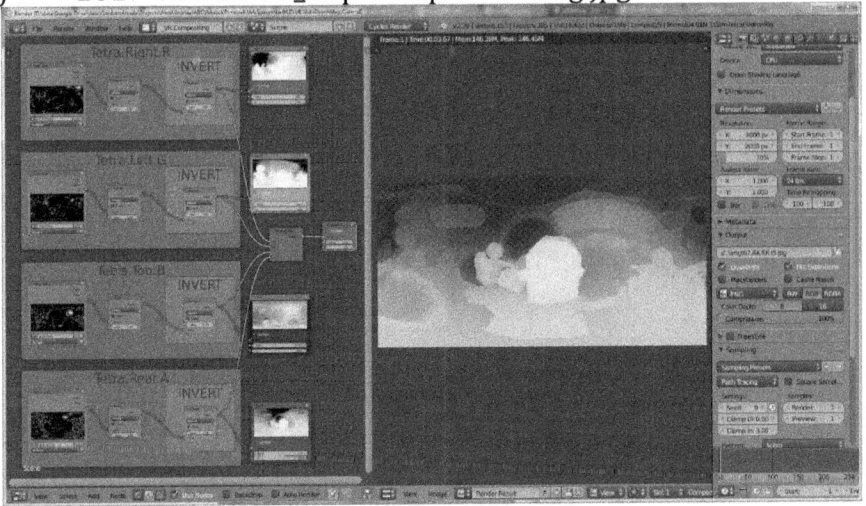

Figure 9: four depth maps using RGB and the alpha channel

d) 2017-01-21d.VR_DepthmapTextureOverUnder.jpg (how it would be saved to be processed by the VR viewer in real time - this is a fake image with no real transparency).

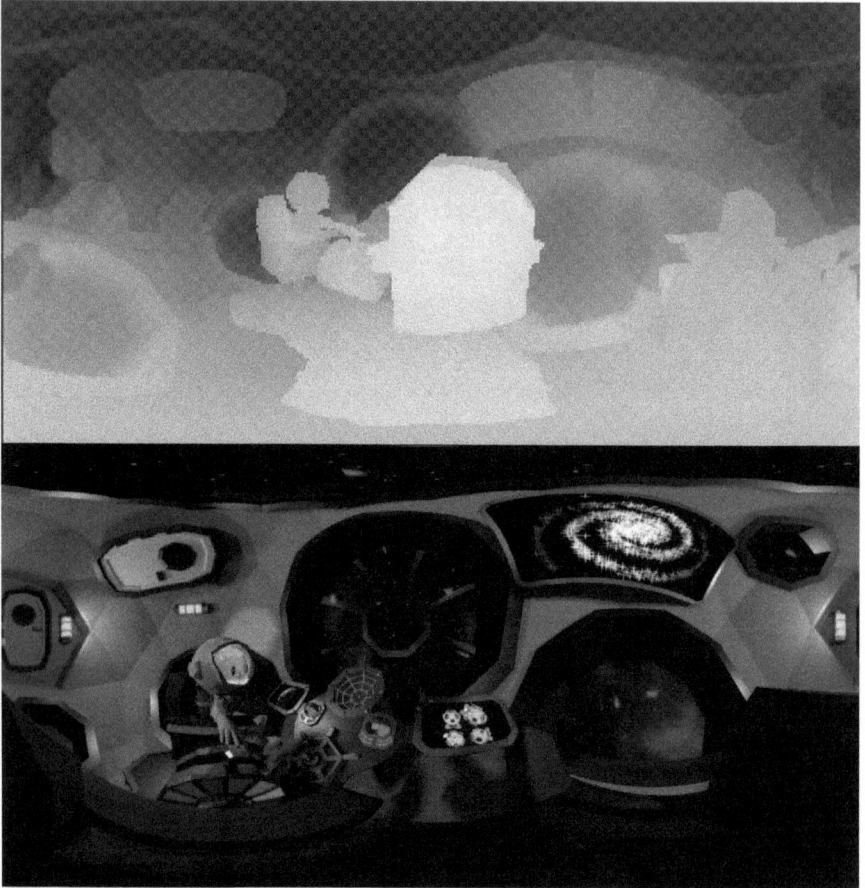

Figure 10: top: the resulting RGBA PNG file, bottom: The photosphere texture

Thank you for thinking this through with me!

Kind regards

Chuck Ian Gordon

--- 8< ------------------------------------

Pyramid encoding: another emerging idea is a better compression of equirectangular or cubemap images in a pyramid encoding. Check out this clever article that explains it in depth: Pyramid Encoding Article at code.facebook.com[23] In short: we can save a lot of storage space if we look at a square in front of us sitting on one corner. We look at the floor of a stretched pyramid which encloses our head with the tip of the pyramid behind our head. We just need to remap our projection onto the pyramid and then unfold it and do a bit of squeezing of the triangles to get a complete square which quite effectively stores all the information.

Google Spotlight stories: I thought a while about whether I would rate Google Spotlight stories as realtime 3D or as hybrid format. You should check the video "Special Delivery" by Aardman on YouTube[24]. To produce a spotlight story you create your animated 3D scene enriched by some special content like events and triggers and send Google an alembic file which is a 3D exchange format. Google processes it and you can enjoy the result in VR in realtime 3D with the spotlight stories app. But often the video is then rendered to a YouTube VR video so you can enjoy it in YouTube without a special app (with the known restrictions unless Google enhances YouTube itself to render realtime 3D).

Conclusion

Now we have traveled the three rivers of rendering and examined some aspects of them. Those examples show: it is important to understand the difference between the various render options (pre-rendered, realtime 3D and hybrid) and their consequences in the viewing experience as well as in the production of your VR content.

---

[23] https://code.facebook.com/posts/1126354007399553/next-generation-video-encoding-techniques-for-360-video-and-vr/

[24] https://youtu.be/XiDRZfeL_hc

We can hope the jungle opens up and we can soon see the clearing, as all that we discussed here will sooner or later be put into standard formats, and then we will need to worry less about this. Yet it is a good idea to have some deeper understanding of the underlying principles because some differences will remain so that is why we took this ride.

We haven't talked about spatial sound yet which is awfully important as it is responsible for about 50% of the presence effect. So, we will continue with spatial sound in the next chapter.

Check your carpet-belt again and follow me to the magic kingdom of sound.

Level 5: Spatial Sound

"The sound and music are 50% of the entertainment in a movie."

George Lucas

Now, VR movie makers welcome to Level 5. Hold on to your carpet while we approach this giant half-transparent head. On the way there I will give you a brief introduction.

Spatial sound isn't new. In fact, I came across it when I designed my first virtual worlds back in 1998 using VRML. It was wonderful. The browser plugin called Cosmo Player did all the work, I just placed sound sources in my VRML file and that was it. Then you had great spatial stereo sound when navigating the 3D world with your laptop, much like normal game engines do today.

I guess this is what every movie maker likes. Just define it and it works. We are getting closer to this goal but we are far from being there. So, let me start with some reading tips and some advice.

I encourage you to read the following excellent articles on spatial sound - we will cover parts of it: The excellent and interesting article by Boris Smus about spatial sound and WebVR[25] (including links to resources to test stuff yourself). A great article from Google[26] introducing the concepts of spatial audio in depth. And for reference (which probably will evolve more or less quickly) - the technical description for the requirements of YouTube's spatial sound format[27].

Also, worth checking out is Google's Omnitone[28]. It is an implementation of a FOA (first-order-ambisonic) decoder with binaural rendering written in Web Audio API.

And my advice: if you are doing a professional production, grab some budget and go and hire an expert for spatial sound. It is a universe that is awfully complicated and yet fascinating, but you can spend ages in getting it right yourself.

But let's get a bit deeper into details. We are almost there. Let me ask you some questions.

The importance and the budget share of sound

Do you know what percentage of the immersive effect of an experience sound is responsible for? Roughly 50%. It plays a key role in VR drawing the user's attention to something. Next question: do you know what percentage of the budget of a classic film production is spent on sound compared to visual special effects? I will give you a hint. It is way less than 50%. (Because I myself was asked, I did a little research. I found numbers ranging from two to five percent and slightly above – depending whether music was also included.) Fascinating, isn't it. Last question: what

---

[25] http://smus.com/spatial-audio-web-vr/

[26] https://developers.google.com/vr/concepts/spatial-audio

[27] https://support.google.com/youtube/answer/6395969?hl=en&co=GENIE.Platform%3DDesktop&oco=1

[28] https://opensource.google.com/projects/omnitone

do you believe will be the average percentage spent on sound in a VR project? ... Make an educated guess or look at some numbers in real projects over the next few years. Did I mention that I am working on an immersive musical? I encourage you to experiment with this budget split factor for spatial sound in your work.

Now we have reached the giant head and gone into orbit. From here you can see the brain through the transparent material and how it reacts to the noise our carpet produces (after I have disabled the silent mode by pressing this button here: klick ... vroooom ...). I will have to continue a bit more loudly so you can still hear me. Look at the head's eyes. They are following us. See the brain activity? What is happening here? Well, a lot. Where do we start?

Directions and Reflections

Sound usually comes from a sound source unless it is ambient - meaning it surrounds you. We have two ears. The brain processes the fact that the sound arrives earlier at one ear than at the other. So, the listener gets a hint as to whether it comes from left or right. This is stereo. But this doesn't tell us whether a sound is coming from the right, from the front or is coming from behind us. This is computed by our brain when we turn our head slightly or move it and this happens instinctually. Another important part of what our brain does is processing multiple reflections of the same sound. There are what are called interaural time differences, interaural level differences and a spectral filtering done by our outer ears. Sound, for example, is sent to our ears directly, reflected from the floor, another part reflected from the floor and then from the ceiling, then from our shoulder, then from parts of our ear. All those different reflected and un-reflected waves pass into our ears. Each reflection changes the sound waves by the nature and texture/fabric of the material that reflects it. Wool reflects sound differently than a mirror, steel or stone, sand or dust. This gives us a sense of where we are even when we close our eyes - a small chamber, a church, a forest. Now, if the sound in the experience stutters, comes from the wrong direction or simply doesn't sound right, it is disturbing or can even destroy the illusion of immersion.

Doppler effect

When we move or when a noisy object moves there is a Doppler effect. Do you remember the last time an ambulance passed you? You could guess the speed of it by the amount the frequency changed. This is an important tool for spatial sound. I remember the movie "A Knight's Tale" where the heroes come back to London. The camera flies over a church and you unexpectedly hear this Doppler effect. This was a wow moment for me. So, in general the Doppler effect increases realism and is usually handled well by game engines like Unity3D automatically. However, it may not always be what you want. In the article from Boris Smus I linked to before, Boris notices that he found the Doppler effect disturbing when he created a spatial music setup. So, as frequently happens, it depends whether you prefer realism or a certain kind of artificial setup to improve the experience for your audience. If we talk about realism, also take into account that sound in movies is usually enhanced compared to reality. Gunfire sounds much louder, richer and deeper than in reality, maybe you want to hear explosions in the space of Kung-Fu-swishes – even if it is unrealistic – just because we are used to it from many movies we have seen. Just consider what emotions, what feelings, you want the audience to experience when designing the sound for your VR movie.

HRTF = Head related transfer functions

When you wear headphones with a VR headset you need the system to translate the sources of sound as you turn and move your head. A sound that comes from the left for example must change its position in your headphones to the front when you turn your head left. This should be done automatically by your "playback" software (game engine, WebVR, VR video player or whatever). If you use another projection method, like for example, a digital fulldome there mustn't be a HRTF calculation, because the sound remains in position while the audience can turn their heads into different directions simultaneously.

Ambisonics

While the software must ensure the correct position of the individual sounds at playback time you have to design the surrounding sound. When designing a fixed-story-line-experience, or providing spatial background sound, you can create ambisonics, which describes a sound sphere with many loudspeakers to simulate spatial sound. Within a (partially) interactive experience this must be done in real time by the game engine by placing spatial sounds correctly.

Recording spatial sound

Recording spatial sound is often described as binaural recording due to the binaural nature of our ears. We spoke about the importance of sound reflections from parts of our ears. There are microphones using heads with soft rubber ears to realistically record binaural sound for humans. This is not enough for VR or AR as it binds the recording to a fixed head position. So, we need more microphones or a so called ambisonic microphone to capture the sound of an environment in 3D. Innovation is also fast here, so check out current microphones. Today we could mention ambisonic microphones like the SoundField ST450, TetraMic, Zoom H2n or the Sennheiser AMBEO VR Mic.

Processing ambisonic sound in your DAW

Check whether your sound software - also often referred as DAW (Digital Audio Workstation) can process ambisonic sound. Often the software vendor provides a plugin to run effects on it, change its position and volume and remix it.

Design a spatial soundscape in your 3D game engine

If your VR or AR experience is interactive, or even to prerecord a sophisticated spatial soundscape to use later as ambisonic sound, you can design your spatial sound in a game engine or by using WebVR for example. There are some rules to obey here. For example: for sounds emitted by an object use mono sounds without echo effects. Why? Let's say it is a dripping water outlet. It will sound differently depending on whether it is outside at a farm, inside a small chamber or in a gigantic cathedral or cave. The playback engine/game engine has to deal with the echo effect on it. It was a bit of a surprise for me first but soon it was totally logical that video card manufacturers like Nvidia that use their capability of raytracing or pathtracing 3D objects also use it explicitly for calculating accurate soundscapes to simulate sound reflections in real time. As of writing this chapter in spring 2017 you will have to use the vendor specific API or SDK to access all of its benefits, but I assume this will be made easier in the future by offering standards like the just launched OpenXR standard.

Test often, test hard, test intensively

As a mismatch between the spatial sound and the visual experience can destroy the immersion instantly you should test your experience intensively. Visit every location your audience might. Use several setups for output (several headphones, stationary surround sound, room scale setups with 6 degrees of freedom, rotational tracking only, ...) and check for consistency. A noisy road without synchronously moving cars damages or even breaks the illusion.

Double check technical stuff when outputting or converting

I was surprised when a sound I recorded for a video suddenly had a metallic distortion which wasn't in the original recording. It turned out it was the transformation with the VLC media player from webm format to mp4. So, include various check stages, keep your original files to go back to if necessary and check the technical specifications of platforms you upload to closely, like the one I linked to above outlining the technical requirements for spatial sound with YouTube VR.

Conclusion

Now traveler on the magic carpet. We have learned and seen that spatial sound is awfully important and quite complex at the same time. What you need to do depends a lot on the nature of your experience (headsets, dome projection, ...) and your playback tools (game engine, VR video player, AR projection, ...). Keep quality high here. If in doubt hire an expert on spatial sound.

Now you may all pass on to the next level.

Level 6: Lessons learned so far

"Some lessons can't be taught, they simply have to be learned."

Jodi Picoult, American Writer

Welcome to Level 6. You can all land your magic carpets. Now look ahead, you and Player One and Player Two. Before you lies the minefield of exploration. Be careful when you proceed. Those who failed before you left tombstones with their lessons learned. So, learn from the pioneers and be extra careful as soon as you don't find any more tombstones. This is the undiscovered country where you yourself are the pioneers to learn some new lessons. Now move on. The first one reaching the other side alive wins.

Suddenly Player Two runs away passing some tombstones quickly. He passes the 4th stone, the 5th, BOOOOOOM. Player Two is gone. You and Player One look at each other and move on. Slowly, carefully and read the text on the first stones.

The tombstone in front of you states:

Practice extensive user testing - because users don't react as expected.

Users in VR simply don't behave as planned by the director. They use their freedom to choose many possible and unconceivable actions and reactions. Many of them don't turn their head much. Most people stay within an angle of 50%, even if your VR experience tells them to turn around, look up or down. So, it is important to do a lot of user testing with your target group. You may be able to outsource a part of the testing. I met Geoff Skow, the founder of FishbowlVR (virtually), when I moderated a panel at the first VR Analytics web summit. They offer VR testing as a service. Anyway, I suggest that you do your own testing and listen closely to your testers. This is also a good reason to set up some Virtual or Augmented reality analytics, to be able to record and replay what people looked at in 3D space, to check what actions they took and what paths they did and didn't follow. It is an awfully important tool to optimize your VR experience upfront. And it also gives you the ability to collect VR Analytics data later after launch to see how the masses react and decide what to improve for future projects. It also might be that the data you collect is valuable in other places so that you can additionally monetize this behavioral data, especially if it isn't possible to connect it to other people's personal profile data. Anyway, you should be aware of different privacy laws around the globe and prepare for some resistance. So, make sure your financial success doesn't solely rely on collected usage data.

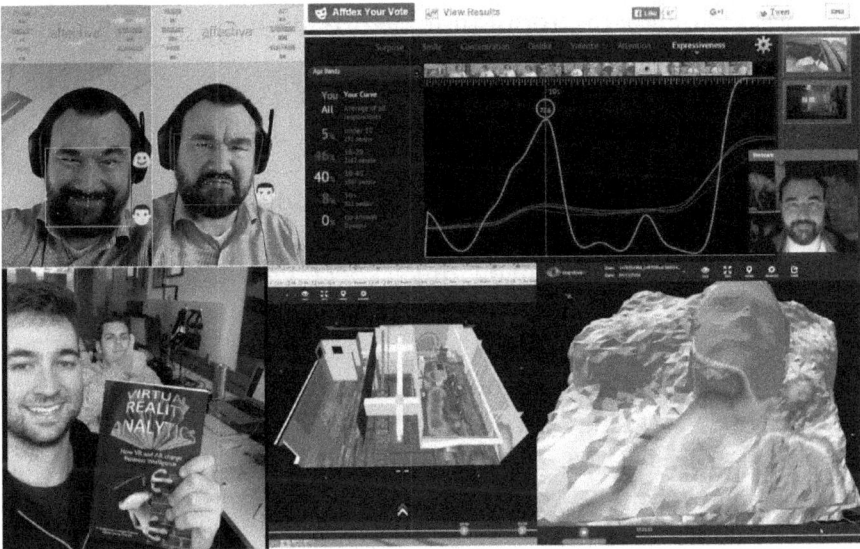

Figure 11: top: own experiments with Emotion Analytics from affectiva, bottom: Robert Merki from CognitiveVR with my book "Virtual Reality Analytics" plus VR Analytics examples (right own scan with 3D heatmap)

You move on. The writing on the next tombstone reads:

The Cinematic VR Formula

Placing or removing an avatar affects the audience.

If we have a fulldome projection with many people you can see there is no point in creating a common avatar which you are the head of. So, a fulldome version of your experience might differ in this point from a VR headset experience. (By the way, this is also true for interactivity. It isn't possible for half the people to choose to attack the goblin while the other half runs away.) Let's assume your audience is wearing a headset. It makes a difference whether they have an avatar body or not. It changes their feeling about the scene and their awareness of their physical presence. Try to use and to remove your avatar. Also, it is important that your avatar is synced to your body feelings. If you raise your hand and your avatar doesn't but the virtual hand remains on your virtual knee this feels odd and breaks the presence. Hand controllers or other tracking options like depth-camera-based hand tracking helps. I believe it is only a matter of time before full body avatars will be a standard we can switch on and off.

There is a difference between the audience just watching in 360° what is happening in camera and being in someone's mind and having a body. Here a good technical solution to creating a believable body experience is key. I just came across a game on the Sony PS VR that solved this aspect very well. It is called Scavengers Odyssey and comes in a bundle called "VR worlds". While you are seated inside a walking mech droid, and have your arms attached to the arms of your chair, your body (chest, arms) reacts when you change your head position and rotation. It uses an inverse kinematics approach (IK) which prevents you from looking at the place where your head is fixed to your chest because your chest naturally moves with you. It gave me a very good believable sense of this virtual body so that I accepted it as my own. If you have the chance, check out the game. But be careful. It is a great example of a good avatar solution, but the rotating jumps in space from one asteroid to another may cause nausea (although they have incorporated some tricks already like narrowing the field of view when jumping to minimize this).

The Cinematic VR Formula

Using objects and frames of reference - makes a difference for nausea/motion sickness.

It's great to ride on a VRcoaster which is a real world rollercoaster where you wear a VR headset and have a ride in an alternative reality. Try it yourself as I did. There are many VR coasters around the world already. See: www.vrcoaster.com . It is great because what you see and what your body feels is in sync so your brain and nervous system can deal with the velocity. What is bad though is having a rollercoaster ride in VR and sitting on a chair or standing without motion. Now your brain gets images that are not matching what your body feels; a good way to make people sick in VR, which we don't want to do, right? If you have (moderate) motion in your experience there is one thing that might help. You can use a frame of reference. That might be a car you sit in, the cockpit of an airplane or spaceship or a deck of a ship. Everything that is like a cage around you helps because it gives you a fixed reference and we are used to such vehicles in real life. It doesn't completely eliminate the problems when moving in VR but it eases the experience.

Moving the camera - lessons learned.

As there is often more than one opinion about a point don't trust anybody but do your own experiments. And consider that you will probably develop some resistance or immunity to motion sickness when practicing often yourself as your brain adapts. So, make sure to test (safely) with less experienced people. Some people have said not to move the camera but that is simply wrong. So, as people didn't get the idea of a moving camera when the first movies were shot, VR experiences will evolve over time as well. Things I found worth thinking about when it comes to a VR camera in motion are:

- keep the horizon horizontal. Let the audience change it by moving their head.

- don't zoom in VR except when using a zoom capable device like a virtual monitor or a virtual spyglass.

- motion is fine but there are some motions that feel more comfortable than others. A constant forward motion seems to work best, as, in reality you don't feel anything (except vibrations and bumps on the road). Accelerating or slowing down should be done carefully. Moving backwards or sideways (strafing) at high speed is not very comfortable. Moving up or down like in an elevator (on a platform with a railing as a frame of reference possibly at constant speed) should be fine. Use ease in and ease out for starting and stopping the elevator. Experiment with quick and slow acceleration durations in your experience.

Guiding the eye - Hey user - look here - noooo - over here - HELLO!

Yes, it is a harsh change for directors. And I also love cutting movies in the way I want, choosing my own framing and having the audience forced to watch what I show. That is why this kind of movie will prevail. But that is not how VR movies work today. We as directors can set up an invitation to the audience for where to look. It is similar to the invitation we create in a theater or in a musical. If you have ever experienced the musical Starlight Express you know that the skaters move around and through the audience on laid out tracks. We also can learn from their creators here. What can we use? Spatial sound of course. And also guiding the eye with light. The VR experience SONAR by Philipp Maas does this in a fascinating way in its opening sequence. A spaceship moves along a dark asteroid and it descends into a hole leading to a cave. You naturally follow the ship because it is using some spotlights and they point to the only interesting areas of the scene. Go and watch it at www.sonar-360.com . Depth of field: blurring things at distances the audience should not look at and focusing on the main point of interest is another method but that is more critical because that is not how our reality works. Instead we focus our eyes on what we want to see and being robbed of this ability might feel odd. If you use it, use it subtly. The first VR headsets with eye tracking intended to use depth of field rendering but this is controlled by the user's eye movement. But as soon as the user controls it it isn't a tool for the director anymore.

Don't scare people in VR unless they want it.

O.K. If you experience a horror story you expect to be scared. But otherwise we shouldn't scare people in VR because we are able to directly trigger their fight-or-flight-response. I was surprised how deep my physical discomfort was during a zombie experience even while I was aware all the time that it was not real. I couldn't persuade my body to have the same insights on the situation. VR directly connects to our brain. Instead find ways to excite people and make them feel comfortable - and sometimes, for a while, you can increase tension with your story, like a good book or movie does. We all should watch for common guidelines and ethics when creating experiences. That being said I am aware that sometimes people need to break rules in order to create a new masterpiece of art. But we should always know the rules beforehand and remember our responsibility for the safety of our audience.

Wow. That was it so far. We passed the last tombstone. Player One has managed it as well. We carefully move on through the undiscovered country toward the next level where we will dive into preproduction.

Conclusion

Relax, director. Yes, VR shifts power from us to the audience. And no, we won't get 100% attention anymore, as theater also doesn't. It's a good opportunity for people to visit your experience twice. Let's re-learn from theater how to guide and influence people. Create a great compelling performance with deep emotion. And then, just let go and relax, director.

Part III

Level 7: - PreProduction Chapter 1: How VR can change preproduction

"By failing to prepare, you are preparing to fail."

Benjamin Franklin

We should remind ourselves that although VR is fed by games and by movies the terminology differs. Especially when it comes to production phases and what is in preproduction, production and postproduction. As we can expect both industries to merge to a certain level we might see these terms also undergo a shift. Here we address everything with the term preproduction that has to happen before the first scene is shot.

We cover preproduction in **three chapters.** First we take a look at how VR can change preproduction of VR movies and of ordinary movies as well. Second we examine the changes VR introduces to classic cinematography (staging, framing, creation of storyboards, rehearsing, ...). Third we take a brief look at the specialty of VR production pipelines.

Let's start with the opportunities of VR in preproduction.

How VR can change preproduction

Let's look at two interesting options that VR offers us for preproduction of VR and non- VR movies: improved location scouting and previsualization in VR.

Location scouting

Many things we describe here are not new. But as the devices to support them are constantly getting cheaper and more powerful they offer additional value at lower cost. Today you can equip yourself easily and affordably for 360° location scouting with 3D scanning using photogrammetry. Of course, you can (and should if you are able to) use high end Lidar technology (laser scanning) which is more accurate and obviously cooler. But let's say you want to make the most out of your location scouting without a huge budget. Grab yourself an affordable 360° camera like a Ricoh Theta[29] or a Samsung Gear 360[30] . Or a stereo version of it like a Vuze camera (as of writing this chapter the Vuze[31] wasn't ready for delivery). Also grab a good camera capable of multi image recordings or video recording. In many cases a good smartphone camera will do.

Now go and shoot a series of 360° stills and maybe some 360° movies. Try to record the exact position of your shots to maybe put them on a map later and have a more complete documentation of the location. Also, if you discover more complex scenes or objects (preferably static scenes without movement) you can record them and create 3D models of them with photogrammetry.

Let's watch how Player One handles the task at hand. (Careful. Practical tech description.)

Player One shoots a lot of 360° stills and puts their position on a custom map of Google Maps. He takes his smartphone cam and records movies from interesting places like a somewhat withered stone wall with some crumbling stairs. Moss and ivy are growing over the place. How romantic and mysterious! While recording the videos Player One moves the camera carefully without abrupt shaking so most of it is sharp and without blurring. At his computer Player One transforms the movie to single jpeg images taking only one out of 24 images from each second. He does that easily within minutes using the

---

[29] https://theta360.com/en/

[30] http://www.samsung.com/us/mobile/virtual-reality/gear-360/gear-360-sm-r210nzwaxar/

[31] http://vuze.camera/

free 3D creation software blender (www.blender.org) which includes a video sequence editor (VSE). So, from one minute's footage he extracts about 60 stills that he uses as input for his photogrammetry program which is Agisoft Photoscan - a commercial, affordable photogrammetry software. The software analyzes features that appear in more than one image and calculates the appropriate camera positions. Then in a workflow with a few steps it calculates a sparse point cloud, next a dense cloud, next creates a mesh and adds a texture. It took Player One some practice and he read many of the how to papers from Agisoft to get better results out of the process. After a while (depending on the power of one's computer) the textured 3d mesh is there and can be exported to a common graphics format for further processing by a 3d software to set up a virtual scene. Thanks Player One!

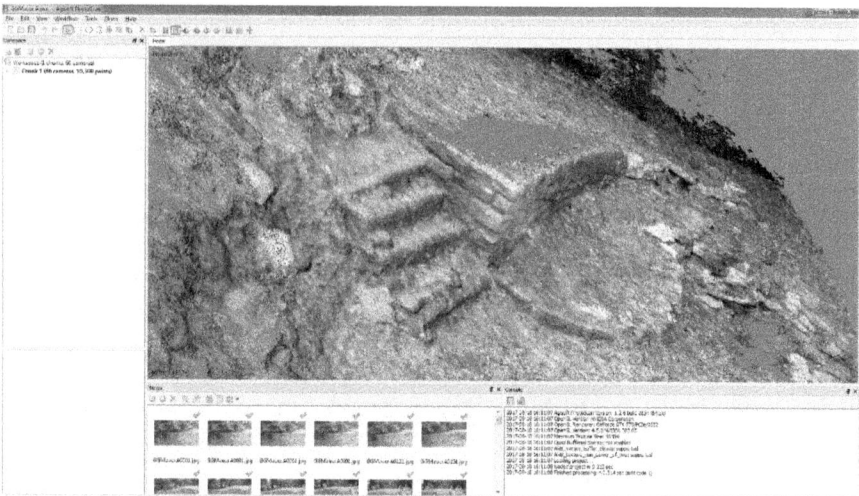

Figure 12: A point cloud I generated with AGISOFT Photoscan from images extracted from a smartphone-video (Google Nexus 5 with HD resolution - I extracted one frame per second) – Location: Gustavsgarten, Bad Homburg at: 50°13'48.8"N 8°35'44.5"E)

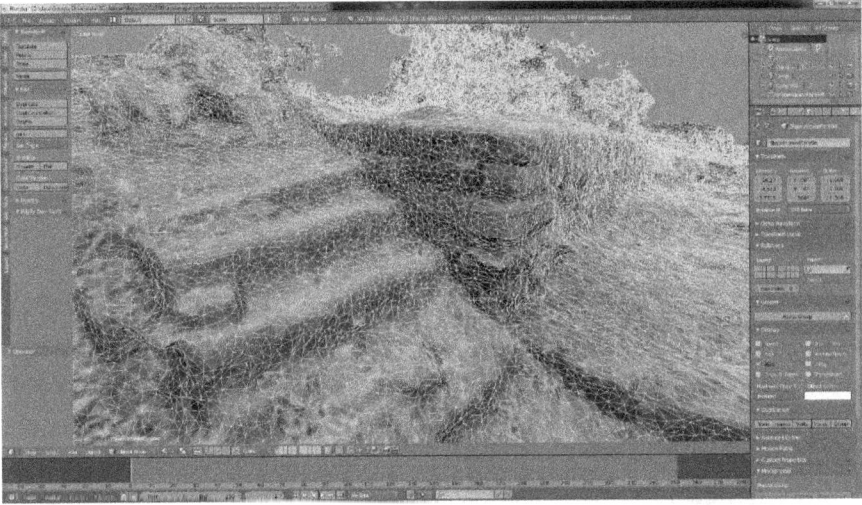

Figure 13: The point cloud converted to a mesh and imported into blender

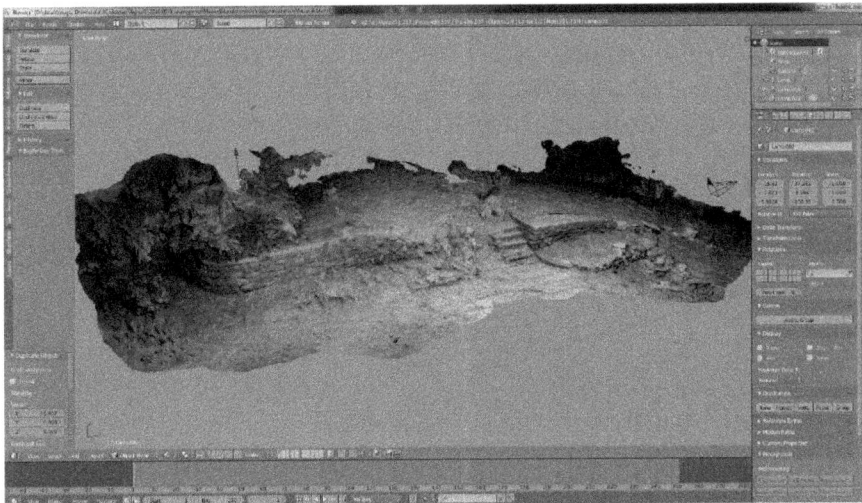

Figure 14: The whole 3D scene in Blender with two point lights

The great advantage of scanning a location is: you can review it in 3D and in VR, conduct physics simulations with it and get a feeling for the location. There are a lot of photogrammetry solutions on the market that come with various pricing models. One interesting solution is Pix4D which can process 360° photos and video and also supports drones. This means you can also scan larger places with 360° cameras by drone and transform whole complex locations like castles, forests with rocks etc. to 3D models. You might want to hire a drone pilot for that or I have already seen drone mapping as a service on the internet. Keep yourself informed about new developments.

Player Two came across the ideal solution. He got a separate high funding round from another gangster boss to be able to afford to borrow some light field recording equipment. Heavy drones outfitted with the latest light field cameras completely scan the interior and exterior of his location by autonomously navigating through it. You can imagine it like the automatic scanning procedure in the movie Prometheus. This solution is converting from science fiction to reality. Right now, it is high price, high complexity but let's give it some time and have another look. We can hope Player Two's box-office-day is so good that he can repay the debt he got into... We shall see.

Spatial scanning and mapping can be done in many ways and is a key technology for a new era in computing platforms that I call USEMIR (Ubiquitous SEnsory MIxed Reality).

VR previsualization with fast and cheap gear

Lately something not so new has experienced a revival - SLAM – Simultaneous Localization and Mapping[32].

It is a key component for advanced Augmented or Mixed Reality content like Microsoft HoloLens applications or just recently for Apple's ARKit and Google's ARCore (vision based) or Tango technology (enhanced with Time of Flight Cameras). Also, it is important for autonomous vehicles. Maybe it's an over-simplification but you could think of it like photogrammetry in real time. The key lesson is: we will have more and more options to affordably 3D scan environments to use them during location scouting or later for previsualization and simulation of scenes.

---

[32] https://en.wikipedia.org/wiki/Simultaneous_localization_and_mapping

The opportunity to 3D scan locations also gives us the chance to quickly previsualize a scene setting in real life size. Some technical things have to be considered. For example, you should limit or reduce the polygon count of your 3D scene to allow better performance in VR with high end or even mobile headsets. Your 3D creation suite should be capable of automatically reducing the polygons of your scanned objects. It may be that you combine multiple scans into one scene. If you take care of mesh integrity (waterproof meshes) and possibly combine several parts you can even run physics simulations (like water waves rolling in) or cars/planes/other objects crashing into your location. But even if the scene isn't perfect it gives you a great sense of presence and the atmosphere of that place. A good start for lower budgets is to grab some 3D software like a blender to do the 3D combination and re-modeling and then to throw it into your favorite game engine (like Unity or Unreal).

If you can obtain high or unlimited budgets you can create for yourself a previz VR cave like ILM XLab did. It is quite impressive how they combine real time lighting and rendering with live motion capture of actors to represent movie characters. Take a look here: star wars at ILMxLabs[33] and Watch their video on youtube[34].

Conclusion

The combination of various techniques today allows us to affordably 3D scan locations and previsualize them in VR. Now let's compare classical and VR cinematography (storyboarding, staging, framing) and then have a look at building a VR production pipeline.

---

[33] http://ilmxlab.com/

[34] https://www.youtube.com/watch?v=7T9Dv1aLMbw

Level 7: - PreProduction Chapter 2: VR Cinematography

"This is a new medium. It's an unwritten canvas. People can figure out what a story looks like and an audience can see if they like it. It's a really unique time."

Chris Milk, Founder of VRSE

Let's compare some aspects of classical movie cinematography and cinematography in VR. If you haven't done already I recommend reading the excellent sources I listed at the beginning of this book, especially: "Film directing shot by shot".

Staging and framing

In movies we do have a frame. So, we do need to stage everything that is visible but not more. Sometimes we do this for providing better lighting or for giving the actors a better sense of presence in the scene. But we don't usually need to construct a whole 360°x180° set. In VR we have to as there is no frame. At least virtually. We may work with darker areas but it is not an option for many films to have spots of attention and everything else being black. You can do one or two movies like that as an art form, but in general people want to experience a rich environment in VR.

We already addressed the question of using an avatar or not and what abilities it has in the previous chapter. This also makes a difference for your staging and for your story dynamics.

Depending on how freely people or their avatar can move in a scene or even an open environment there are three options. You either have to craft more objects of the scene in more detail (to provide an unchallenged presence even if the audience closely examines an object at the edge of your scene). Or you limit the audience's freedom of movement by some believable obstacles or rednecks with broad shoulders. Or, the third option is to create parts of the scene procedurally like was popular in the past few years (although it is not new. It was used in computer games I

72

played in my youth back in the 1980s - to mention Elite on my C64 for example). Anyway, you should help your audience with some sort of optical indicator or with an accompanying character in what direction to look for the center of action in case they get lost.

VR storyboarding

A traditional movie storyboard represents the frame you see on screen transferred to a piece of paper. As we have a complete surround look this isn't easily done with VR. The question is: how do you represent the whole scene on a 2D medium? I came across a variety of approaches. Each has some advantages and some disadvantages. As often there is a tradeoff between accuracy and mood, between ease of creation and ease of understanding the scene. Here are some examples I came across. The names I mostly made up myself. Please refer to the original sources in case you want to accurately name them

Vincent McCurley's Article on VR Storyboarding

There is a well written and illustrated article about VR storyboarding[35] from Vincent Mc Curly. He represents the action with a (somewhat isometric) 3D view from behind and above giving you some impression of a 3rd person perspective like you know from video games. The author separates the scene into different areas by natural viewing angles. First an angle you can view in without moving your head, second an angle of view you can achieve by turning your head without moving your shoulders. On the distance dimension he separates the scene by distances where things are too close, where things can be excellently observed by eye-only-stereoscopic vision and where things are too far for stereo sensing by eyes only. I would doubt the given far distance. It might be appropriate for VR headsets in 2015 to 2017, but as time passes and VR resolution increases I believe the distance to be further away. We could cross check this by the information I gave earlier. If our fovea is capable of recognizing

---

[35] https://virtualrealitypop.com/storyboarding-in-virtual-reality-67d3438a2fb1

60 pixels per degree everything that makes less difference and therefore doesn't change one pixel is indistinguishable to us. The rest is math (rule of three / intercept theorems).

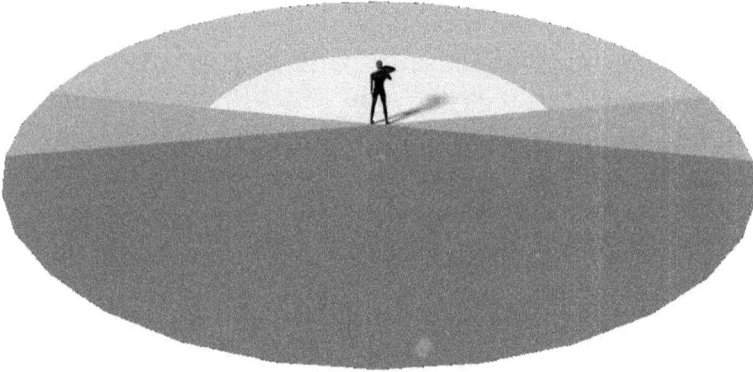

Figure 15: VR Storyboard as proposed by Vincent McCurly (own 3D reconstruction by Chuck Ian Gordon)

The opened tin or opened can

If you are inside a cylinder/can/tin and open the top and the bottom and cut the can from top to bottom on one side you can get a can projection. Brad Herman, formerly head of Dreamlab at DreamWorks explained this in his famous talk at the FMX 2015 in Stuttgart. You see everything around you. At the same time the wall of the can is slightly shifted. Probably to prevent people right behind the protagonist being cut in half. The area was split into 3 distances: a personal space where the audience can reach things with their arms; an action space where the action of the scene happens, and a vista space that just provides the visible environment which is not part of the action.

Figure 16: A VR Storyboard using a cylinder projection which reminds me of an opened can

The radar storyboard

Crytek, the creators of the Cryengine and the Filmengine (which especially is dedicated to VR movie making) showed an elegantly simple and intuitive approach at the FMX 2016. It is a combination of a front screen view with a radar view from the top. This is quite similar to traditional storyboards plus the radar circle that duplicates some information. The radar screen also shows the angle of the framed screen. It seems to me that this is an easy way to create storyboards for VR quickly that can be understood easily.

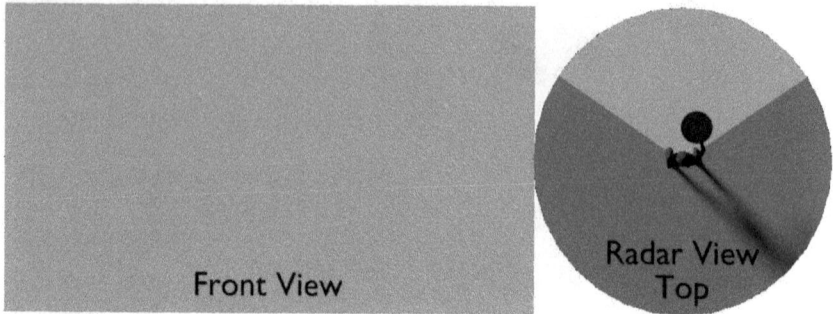

Figure 17: A radar storyboard representation. Left: The front view (like your movie screen), right: The radar top view. The light part is what you see in the front view

3dimensional VR storyboards

It takes a bit more effort to saddle up but why not use 3D storyboards? Once you have simple versions of your assets available you can easily place them in 3D software and even quickly create simple keyframe animations that give you the chance to quickly create a VR story reel which is an animatics version of your scene with the correct timing. There are several ways to do this. I will mention some. Every 3D creation suite should be capable of staging objects and characters and exporting them to a format that a game engine can use so you can easily view your storyboard in VR. An example is: model and animate keyframes in Blender, export to fbx and import this into Unity. In this way you also can keep your .blend files. Unity can process them, but in the end it just calls Blender in the background and uses it to do the fbx conversion for you.

Figure 18: My own 3D storyboard representation

Another option I want to mention also uses Blender. It provides a function called grease pencil where you can easily draw in 3D space and even animate your drawings. There have been some great enhancements of grease pencil lately and filmmakers use it to even produce complete animated movies.

Create your scene in VR

With the HTC Vive and Google TiltBrush you can create 3D drawings. Your scene can grow to be really huge as you are able to teleport yourself. There are some artists creating wonderful walkable scenes with TiltBrush. You can check out many of them at sketchfab.com. TiltBrush can export .fbx which can be directly uploaded to Sketchfab.

Besides TiltBrush there is a growing number of solutions for 3D modeling, painting and sculpting directly in VR. Check it out frequently as it might provide great solutions for VR storyboarding. I recently tried an early access version of VIRTUAnimator for the HTC Vive. It enables you to stage a scene with objects and characters, pose them with keyframes or even record your manipulation in real time. This enables you to control an inverse kinematics avatar like you're a puppeteer. When you get into the right position it is like a partial motion capture. Some videos show people using two additional Vive trackers attached to their shoes with an inverse kinematics avatar for real time room- scale motion capture at a way lower price than classic mocap studios.

All these developments let me imagine that VR storyboarding and VR animatics will move more and more from pencil and paper (or tablets) to VR space.

One side thought here: you can use VR and VR storyboards to tell a story in VR. But if you grant yourself the luxury of creating everything in VR/360° you can later choose the best angles for your screen version of the movie. To quote Patrick Osborne, the director of Pearl[36] - the first VR movie nominated for an Oscar: "I wish I could make every film in VR first and find the shots later, it's such a luxury!" he says. "I've become more of a VR evangelist. Especially when it comes to creating artwork in VR. TiltBrush and Quill have changed the game for me when it comes to designing worlds."

Lessons to re-learn from theater for VR movies

What has classic theater to do with VR storyboarding? The VR storyboard/-storyreel/-animatics represent your story on a timeline and defines your cut scenes. Cutting, timing and scene length differ in VR and will also evolve over time with the advancement of cinematic VR experiences. Today we can take into account these lessons: people need (some) more time in VR to orient and understand the scene. Cutting in VR is slower - the takes are longer - as are the takes in reality. This also means if there is acting or dialog it usually is longer in VR than in movies where you cut often and can create a beautiful dialog from mosaic pieces cut together even if the actor was barely able to remember a whole sentence. Well, if you animate then of course you can cut

---

[36] https://www.theverge.com/2017/2/26/14738098/oscars-2017-google-pearl-spotlight-story-patrick-osborne-vr

the sounds to a brilliant 10 minute speech and it may look natural. But if you film a real scene your actors will have to perform longer takes without interruption. Like... yes. Like in theater. The rehearsal of theater plays demands different approaches for the actors than for movies with short cut scenes. And this is also something you have to consider when populating your VR storyboard and planning the flow of your story. This also has an impact on your (rehearsal- and shooting) budget. So, here it is also important to keep track of time and costs and to optimize calculation frameworks and templates for future projects.

Conclusion

For staging VR, planning and rehearsing we can re-learn a lot from theater and on-stage musicals, some of them already quite immersive like Starlight Express where audience and actors are interwoven. This transfers to VR storyboards, VR-storyreels/-animatics. VR storyboards demand some significant changes to traditionally framed storyboards. At the same time new developments open up a lot of chances to create for, and in, VR in new natural ways, like painting or constructing your storyboard scenes in VR and puppeteering or motion capturing for your VR-storyreel/VR-animatics. In the next chapter we will have a closer look at building a VR production pipeline.

Level 7: - PreProduction Chapter 3: The VR Production Pipeline

"What is it like to walk in someone else's shoes? Books allow us to imagine it, and movies allow us to see it, but VR is the first medium that actually allows us to experience it." Nick Mokey - from his underline at digital trends[37].

Well... this chapter might provide more challenges to write than I thought. I think mainly because of several interconnected layers

---

[37] https://www.digitaltrends.com/features/dt10-we-have-virtual-reality-whats-next-is-straight-out-of-the-matrix/

of moving targets that we face here. But as we are not alone and you and Player One and Player Two will accompany me with this let's start. Since 2012 I figured out how to create a production pipeline for a holodeck movie. And I discovered: there is no such thing as the one and only best solution. Movie production pipelines have developed some standards but as technology advances rapidly they are constantly subject to change. The other reason is: the best solution for your VR movie depends on the scale of your project, the budget, and parts depend on the output you want to create. Let's huddle up at the campfire and make a plan. Player One: you get this fine book I have already recommended for movie production pipelines: "production pipeline fundamentals for film and games" by Renee Dunlop. Player Two: you can have a closer look at this book: "The Art of Game Design: A Book of Lenses" by Jessie Schell. Depending on the kind of your project, your production pipeline might be more similar to a production pipeline for games or for movies. Either way I think of it as an ordinary games/movie production pipeline that is extended by some VR aspects. So, we will focus on those extensions as the recommended books give a very solid foundation already and there is no point in duplicating them.

From lessons learned to pipeline principles to a pipeline

If you create 3D scenes and animate them you will have some common building blocks in the first part of your production pipeline, whether the output is going to be a game or/and a prerendered movie. From the lessons learned so far we can derive some principles that will lead our way before actually implementing them. Here are some that seem important to me (although some of them should be common sense in software projects anyway - and movie and game creation are software projects):

Figure 19: Checklist for a VR production pipeline

- **use loosely coupled systems**

It might be necessary and a good idea to use many components and integrate them in automated workflow. Not only because it creates a beautiful mosaic but because certain results often require special best of breed components that might even change during production phases. So, it is important to be able to quickly bring in new components or rearrange them rapidly. The best way to do this is loosely coupling systems without getting trapped in oversized service oriented architectures. There are many interesting and practical approaches (of which some of them are quite old) that can help here. From JSON over RESTful services, Microservice architectures and more. This is not an IT architecture book but you should have a look at that stuff or have some professional IT architects in your team to help build you such an infrastructure.

- **use simple, text based, powerful systems that can be scripted**

Yes there are nice graphical tools to achieve a lot. But my experience in large scale software projects over the past few decades is: when you need power, extreme flexibility and mass data processing with high performance, the best thing is to stick to program code, scripts and the power of command line shells that can be scripted and automated.

- **automate as much as you can**

Sure you can have manual parts in your production pipeline. I stitched the first VR image from pixel columns in a half-automated half-manual process. It took some hours until I had the process set up for one frame. You can't do such a thing with thousands of frames. And you can be certain there will be a lot of rework. So, make sure to automate as much as you can. At least for the second time you do the same thing so that it is automated for when you need to do it the third time.

- **create abstraction tier(s) as intermediate result layers**

It is a good idea to create as much work as possible in intermediate result layers: technology advancement and flexibility for output options that are unknown or unplanned today. Think about using the results you create for a prerendered movie, for a game engine based VR game, for a tablet/smartphone game and for 3D printed and 2D merchandising on T-Shirts, cups, whatever. The more you can create in the common part of your pipeline the better. Also if you have a 3D recorded VR movie you will have some parts that are modeled or processed in 3D. And if you are in the lucky position to use a light field recording system you might use the servers and software that come with the camera equipment plus a 3D compositing solution like Nuke to create 70% of your results with that. So, check all components to see if they could be used in a common part of your pipeline that produces intermediate results. The inputting and receiving systems can then be interfaced to this abstraction layer.

- **use a version control system**

As pipelines undergo a lot of changes it is important to have a version control system in place that helps you find out what versions of modules and stages of your pipeline are compatible with each other.

- **archive your work**

If you stuck to the previous advice you can one day archive your production pipeline and restore it years later for the production of some new content for new formats and media. The more you create loosely coupled systems and good intermediate abstraction layers the easier it will be for you to integrate some components of your then ancient production pipeline to a new one.

- **document extremely well**

In order to manage a complex production pipeline over time you need excellent documentation. You must know which version of 3D objects worked with which version of the lighting and rendering and what exchanged data was compatible between components. This is even more important if you or somebody else unboxes your archive some years later and asks: how the heck does this work and where should I start? Does this good documentation cost you money and time? That depends on your point of view. You have to invest in it at the first production. But you profit from it vastly when somebody wants to make more money out of your assets. So, maybe ask them if they are ready to take personal responsibility for abandoning investment protection so that you can write that down for your meeting minutes for later reference ;-) .

- **include metadata for VR content (e.g. for user testing and VR Analytics)**

Here is an incentive to help you get along again with the guy you just embarrassed. We know that people react differently in VR from what many directors expect. So, we know that we need to do a fair amount of user testing. Therefore, we can use the techniques of Virtual Reality analytics. The data stored and derived from those tests can be reused for profiling and market research and might be interesting to companies who would like to buy behavioral insights. So, this could be an additional source of funding. To get an overview you can read the book we published in 2016 about virtual reality analytics. Just go to amazon.com and search for that term and it will show up.

- **think about virtualization and include them in the archiving process**

Virtualization is a powerful way to react flexibly to changing demands over time. Whether it is complete virtualization of servers or using containers, it can help you when requirements change. Depending on your decision here you might need experts to set up and administrate your virtual environment. Do take this seriously! Worse than an important server failing is when all servers fail and production comes to a standstill because you didn't know how to set up your SAN or something. Of course you also can use systems in the cloud. But you need to make sure that they are secure and can't be accessed by unauthorized people or companies. Finally, don't forget to also include your virtualized environment in your archiving process. It wouldn't be the first time someone can't reconstruct the infrastructure a system ran on after some years. Despite the complexity virtualization offers a great opportunity to do exactly this. Start over where you left a long time ago.

- **be ready to use the power of the cloud e.g. render farms and production partners**

Your system probably won't end up on your premises. You might want to use the power of render farms or involve external companies to do parts of the work. So, you will have to set up a secure (VPN-based) connection and integrate it into your workflow. If it is not commodity stuff they provide, like render farms do, make sure they also follow your guidelines for loosely coupling, documenting and archiving. Maybe put a version of their environment in a safe in trust in case that company is sold or dissolved.

Conclusion

We will cover some more technical aspects in more depth in the chapters about production and postproduction. For now we have covered some principles to be considered when extending your ordinary production pipeline for VR productions. Gather the experts in your existing production pipeline and discuss those principles with them. Bring in some VR experts and find good solutions as one team to boldly build pipelines where no one has done so before.

Time to enter the production stage.

Level 8: - Production

"He hated location. Just hated it. He says, you don't get the right lights. You've got the noise. And you have to then come in and redub. If ever he could get away without location, he would."

> Patricia Hitchcock about her father Alfred Hitchcock who preferred to shoot in the studio whenever possible.

In this level we cover shooting VR in the real world before taking a brief look at purely-animated-VR-experiences.

Shooting VR

The great day has arrived. You shoot in VR today. We will discuss camera options and setups later. Let's start with specialties of scene setups for VR movies. What is different, Player Two?

Player Two: "em. VR is great so we earn lots of money and won't find a wet grave in the harbor..."
Yes thank you. Player One?
Player One: "
- usually the director is not on set and almost nobody of the other crew. Just the scene, the actors, some microphones and the cast.
- we will film in 360°, probably stereoscopic. So, everything visible from the camera is important as the audience can later examine it.
- if we are lucky we can shoot volumetric video to be used to create real 3D scenes in the computer later.
- as we will be cutting less and dialogs last longer the cast has to

prepare and rehearse more like for a theater piece.
- we can also learn a lot from 3D stage building like theaters and musicals do."
Well done, Player One. Everything you said is right. Let's follow up here.

The set without crew and props

There are two options for the invisible film crew. Either you hide props and crew somewhere and peek through tiny holes (which some productions do) or you don't hide them and create a digital overlay later in postproduction with camera matchmoving technology. That means you reversely resolve the exact camera position from your footage (with math that your 3D software should provide) and add (animated) photorealistic 3D objects in postproduction. This especially might be necessary if you have a complex lighting situation with lots of spots you just cannot hide.

Figure 20: To have a cosy scene in VR either the crew and props have to be hidden or they must be eliminated later in postproduction

We will cover this later in the postproduction levels. What is important here: you should have accurate 3D scan data of your scene and you definitely need to collect complete lighting information in the form of HDR spheres to reconstruct lighting later in postproduction. Otherwise your artificial object will look weird in some way. Good news for the director: even if not on set he can use VR just before or even during shooting by using the (stereo) 360° camera in the scene and watch it with a VR headset in your <u>on set video village</u>[38]). So, he gets a personal impression just as the audience will later.

What cameras do we have on set?

Whatever the fate of VR and AR movies will be, there is a lot of new development in the recording sector that creates completely new solutions unthinkable some years ago and this will revolutionize not only VR movies but also ordinary movie production for screens. Let's have a look at the present state. And if you read this some time in the future please don't laugh too loudly as you have this power in your pocket as everybody has. Back in our days those numbers were quite impressive and unusual.

You can shoot in 360° monoscopic. Automatic stitching for this is fairly good. But the immersion is somewhat limited. You can turn to 360° stereoscopic. Stitching is more complex as you would need 3D information for perfect stitching. You might add 3D information by using depth sensors and later combine that data to get better and faster results. The usual way today is that algorithms detect optical similarities and then do the stitching without knowledge of depth. Or you borrow a light field recording system that usually comes with the server equipment at a very high price but gives you a lot of opportunities that may make it worth the investment. Here is some data from my notes from FMX 2015 from the presentation of Lytro Cinema which is not a 360° system but an ordinary movie camera that directly records light field information. This gives you sub pixel information on distance, color and orientation of each point plus some more things like reflection information and therefore tells you something about the material etc. . Here is my data (if I didn't

---

[38] http://filmescape.com/what-is-video-village

87

write down everything completely accurately it should be enough for you to get the point):

---8< ---------

fmx 2016 fri.14:00 Lytro Immerge, computational Cinematography, Jon Karafin (Lytro head of light field video)

Some numbers:
- 300fps (frames per second) at an insane amount of 755 megapixels.
- creates rgba at subpixel level. Immense (color + alpha channel (transparency))
- have hexagon pixel data for everything. 4d plenoptic domain.

Technical Notes:
- computational Cinematography based on computational photography based on computational tomography. Inverse convolution and some math.
- Microlense array in front of a sensor where the sensor would have been breaking the ray into components. With computing you can calculate the position of it in space.
- The sub-apertures e.g six by six create many images from different point of view. Each pixel.
- Lytro ecosystem: cam, server, editing, distribution options (with the light field master you can produce all formats without ever going back in your prod pipeline)
- In the Demo Jon showed: NukeStudio: on set one hour crash course. Everything on set is captured as metadata keyframe.
- Launching Nuke. Node based 3D vfx sw. Manipulate dof (depth of field) in Nuke. You can animate you dof. Proxy mode for quick editing. Final output is better.
- 19*x sub apertures

What you can do with it:

• Chuck Gordon: Means: they can isolate the shot objects without greenscreen (light fields spill suppression) (annotation while writing the book: You can do this also with other depth sensing technologies)- Viametric flow:

shutter angle can be defined later, means you also have full control over your motion blur.

- You can create arbitrary lens parameters (e.g. 3 lens blades instead of 12). So, you can replace the cam after production.

- You can create anamorphic lens at will (free angle) without pixelating.

- Relighting: you have a normal path and xyz coordinates for everything. You can completely re light your scene after production.

- Light field camera tracking: with sub pixel precision of camera tracking. You can completely relocate your camera (unshake shot)

- First shot with confetti and second shot without separated and then recombined.

Q&A:
Lightfield comp tree:
Q1: relation to 3d movies? You completely can define all stereo eye positions you want (Chuck Gordon: Means you can create your 3D movie version almost for free)
Q2: Relation to Lytro Immerge? (Chuck Gordon: Lytro cinema is the screen movie camera while LYTRO immerge is a football/soccer ball sized sphere for directly recording VR surround light fields (planned at that time))
Actual sensor 40,000k for 4k resolution. For 8k resolution working on their next generation.
Less than 120gb per second if you go to 120 fps.
---8< ---------

I have already mentioned this in the chapter: "History, status and future of VR" - to quote myself here: Lytro also announced the Lytro immerge - a ball shaped lightfield camera for capturing live action light fields. (Well we were able to see the first prototype

The Cinematic VR Formula

and it more a 1-by-1-meter array of plenoptic single cameras - nevertheless look at the results of their Halleluja video[39] - we are on the way.)

More news in April 2017: Facebook announced various initiatives to create an AR platform and provides tools for that. One part of this initiative is a cooperation of Facebook working on a 360° depth sensing camera together with OTOY, specialists for realtime rendering. There is an impressive video showing what they can do. Summary: you can freely record, combine, and mix immersive 3D content to give you VR (and AR) experiences with 6 degrees of freedom (also parallax) which we covered already as hybrid approach. Watch this video on YouTube:"OTOY Explains 6 Degrees of Freedom Video Workflow Developed With Facebook"[40]. In this video OTOY refers to ORBX Scene files for the transfer of recordings to your 3D software which is then processed into an ORBX media file to allow consumption with your VR headset and other devices. ORBX.js was developed by OTOY and Mozilla for plugin free video streaming in the browser. In the video at 3minutes, 23 seconds a bunch of formats for processing and distribution is shown including formats for viewing with 6DOF (six degrees of freedom). As development continues you should check this out frequently.

The list doesn't end here. There are more technologies evolving for performance capturing with or without motion capturing ranging from 8i.com over EvE depth sensor capturing from the https://experimental-foundation.com/ to various new ways to do it using depth sensing devices like Google Tango phones or combinations of a Microsoft HoloLens with some camera gear. As development is fast here you need to frequently observe what happens on the market.

---

[39] https://vimeo.com/213266879

[40] https://youtu.be/EK3RaU6IPf4

90

The Cinematic VR Formula

As I said, I don't know where cinematic VR will be in some years. But indicators show that immersive, volumetric recording, playback and interactive animation will play an important role over the next several years. We might think of it as immersive VR/AR/MR cinematography. And even if certain aspects are quite different, many things are common ground. So, maybe later we will create a book about cinematic AR. But why do I think that will happen?

We see many more examples. Apple still quite mysteriously announcing that they see a high potential in AR - and if you look at their company acquisitions (Primesense, Faceshift, ...) you could have come to that conclusion for yourself earlier (which I actually did). As of editing in July 2017 Apple revealed officially their engagement in VR as well as the ARKit which right now doesn't use depth sensors (like Google Tango) but instead uses optical tracking (and probably some AI components) to create quite impressive AR projections (with tablets in the first move). I believe we can surely expect nice head mounted devices to follow. (As mentioned earlier: Google announced its ArCore Technology quickly after that)

Some more thoughts:

What would be the ideal setup for VR recording?

In the intro scene of my novel 3futurez I describe a light field recording scene that is rather nearer future than science fiction. Several light field camera drones are recording the scene. With a tetrahedron setup (4 cameras) you should be able to cover the complete scene. The data is gathered by a computer system close to them and integrated in real time. Unwanted things are cut out - like the other drones or staff at the recording site. Pre-scanned information replaces those patches. From today's point of view nothing of that is unrealistic. It is simply some linear progress that we have to make. By linear I mean there doesn't need to be more breakthrough discoveries. Just a Moore's-law-like-improvement (which in itself is of an accelerating nature) of several technologies: over the air data transfer rates, weight of camera equipment, battery power of drones and camera equipment, processing power of the receiving workstation. All the development we have seen for some time points to the solid expectation that capable technology will be there at affordable prices in the near future.

Make two movies for 1.5 times the budget

Pure VR feature length movies may be considered to be a great financial risk. As we have already pointed out one approach is: create a screen version and a VR/AR version at the same time. Yes this will mean more budget. But it distributes risk and many things can be reused. A large part of the production pipeline. You have the actors right there. Shoot some scene alternatives for the screen and some for VR with a different pace for different cutting. Maybe you will not exactly hit 1.5 times the cost of the movie, but if you don't mess up everything you will be significantly under 2. Record your performance numbers, create post-movie-calculations, review your learnings. The more advanced your recording technology is (the better the live action 3D capture) the more easily you can use shots for both - the screen version and the VR version - even if they vary widely.

Purely-Animated-VR-Experiences

The lines between movie recording and 3D animation are blurring anyway. Today it isn't unrealistic to capture the actors, scan them, rig their 3D models, motion capture them, animate them or the mocap data of stuntmen in scenes where they never were and mix this with animation data using a game engine adding physics simulation to it. You can approach your (VR)movie completely 3D scanning everything, build the rest in 3D and combine it to the finished product. We will have a more detailed look at camera matchmoving later in the postproduction chapter.

I had the pleasure recently to visit the motion capture studio of Metric Minds[41] in Frankfurt, Germany. It is a hall with a large

---

[41] http://metricminds.com/

performance area where up to 14 people can be captured in a scene at once. This is a multi-million-dollar investment but worth it if you want to record complex scenes.

I started working with some nice tools (in an early stage) that allows you to motion capture your performance, your dialogs and create additional animations in VR. These are just examples - the list is neither complete nor does it favor the above mentioned solutions. I just want to give you an idea. Facial Motion capture: you can use <u>Facerig Studio</u>[42] for facial motion capture.

Figure 21: facial motion capture with facerig and my laptop webcam

You can either transfer your recording (or live streaming) onto a predefined 3D character (which isn't the intention of most original VR movie makers), or you can export 3D animation files (.dae or .fbx) and use them with your favorite 3D animation software. There is extensive tech documentation if you want to use the mocap data or if you want to create your own 3D avatar that can work with FaceRig Studio to create your customized live streaming or video recording. For animations in VR you need to

---

[42] https://facerig.com/

rely on the exported mocap data to rearrange it in your 3D software.

There are low cost alternatives as well, like the Ikinema Orion Mocap solution[43] which simply uses a HTC Vive, the hand controllers and some additional trackers from HTC with an inverse kinematics (IK) solver to transform the position and movement data of those components to an IK-rig (a skeleton designed to be animated with inverse kinematics).

Figure 22: Motion capture can be separated and later be rearranged for face, hands and body

Instead of animating everything by hand or motion capture you can create your animation straight in VR itself using VIRTUAnimator[44] for the HTC Vive (early access, available at the steam store for US$9,99 as of July 17th 2017). You can create keyframe animations of characters (and props) by placing the life-sized characters in 3D space and let the computer interpolate the moves. Or you can record it which gives you the ability for some

---

[43] https://ikinema.com/Orion

[44] http://www.virtuanimator.com/

kind of puppeteering e.g. when you get behind the character and wave his hands or other body parts. So, it is some kind of partial mocap or something in between animation by hand and mocap. Even if you have to clean up the results it is an interesting and intuitive way to work.

Another great example I came across is the 20-minute Youtube Video "DIY Kinect Motion Capture Studio | Blender"[45] which uses a Micrsosoft Kinect 2, NI mate[46] and Blender[47] to set up a motion capture home studio. It was provided by Grant Wilk who runs http://remingtongraphics.net/. Actually this process isn't that new. There are many older examples using a Kinect 1 or an Asus Xtion to do the same. But the 20-minute wrap up of the complete process seems quite concise helpful.

One word to prevent a misapprehension. It is true for high end mocap services as well as for self-recorded lower cost variants: usually you will need to clean up, smooth and postprocess your mocap recordings. But in my experience mocap quality is rising so the postprocessing work is getting less over time.

So, as we have already pointed out (and will do so again in the next chapter) now is the time to create new tools in VR and AR that will help us create better VR and AR experiences, as we created new GUI and web tools back in the 1990s that helped us create better and more graphical web experiences back then.

Conclusion

Shooting for VR means capturing and postprocessing reality. What helps tremendously is that you don't just capture a stereo video but also add depth information. With that you enrich the possibilities of manipulating your recording profoundly. And you will need that to hide crew and props on set or to combine

---

[45] https://www.youtube.com/watch?v=1UPZtS5LVvw

[46] https://ni-mate.com/

[47] https://www.blender.org/

different real and virtual parts for amazing scenes. The latest developments in immersive recording equipment point to a glorious future where we can easily and freely combine all sorts of stuff to create the dream worlds we want to show the audience. So, now we are ready for the next level - postproduction.

Level 9: - PostProduction

"I think VR is one of the most exciting areas in the industry today, with potential to influence how we consume content for generations to come."

Jen Dennis, head of RSA VR,
the VR Division of Ridley Scott's RSA Films[48].

I just returned from FMX 2017 - the annual event of Europe's Movie, games and VFX industry. It was great again and fully packed with four days of the latest innovations and trends in VR and AR. If you have the chance, go there it is an awesome place to get inspiration and to network. What became clear this year was this:

First: Volumetric recording and editing (no matter with what technology) is becoming commonplace (although right now gear and software are expensive and processes and formats are proprietary and in the early stages). The clear goal is to provide 6 degrees of freedom (6DoF) for the audience which really increases the immersion (presence) immensely.

Second: The boundaries between preproduction, production and postproduction are continuously blurring, those phases are merging more and more. We see a lot of work done in parallel iteratively. Previz in VR is widely used in VR and non-VR productions. While some people create a scene they already use raw models that are refined and optimized in parallel in real time

---

[48] https://uploadvr.com/ridley-scott-vr-studio/

by other teams. Having everything in 3D becomes more and more important.

Third: Building VR in VR: I have seen more and more examples of tools that allow people to build their VR experience right in VR. It may be storyboarding, puppeteering, creating scenes or applying materials. Where it speeds up development and gives us a better emotional impression of a scene early on we will use more VR (and AR) tools to create and refine immersive content. (We covered some examples for this in the production chapter before.)

That being said, let's use the well-known structure that bundles postproduction (simply put: everything that happens after shooting) to discuss some important aspects. We could go very deep technically here with each aspect. But as many workflows and processes are subject to change in the future due to fast-paced development, we will rather cover the basics so you can get actual tech specs from specialized sources at the time you are reading this.

Figure 23: Post production is more and more merging with preproduction and production

cutting in VR (closing the eye)

Yes, you can cut in VR. But be clear that it disrupts the experience, especially when it is a hard cut without relation to the story. What has proved to work well is using an eye blink, meaning to turn black quickly and then more slowly "opening the eye" again meaning to raise the black from bottom to top. The whole blink can occur in about 1/5th of a second or 0.2 seconds. Between blinks you can, for example, teleport people to a close location, display a menu and so forth. People are getting used to teleport in VR so this may become commonplace if you need it. Other ways of good cutting include: the use of obscuring objects, e.g. the audience can see a boy walk through a forest. He passes by behind a tree and behind that tree he converts to a grown up; magical/dimensional portals, where appropriate and matching the story, a magical or dimensional portal with a fade to blurry colorful or white can be used to change scenes without the problem of disorientation. But as mentioned: it must match the story. Otherwise a soft blending effect may be a good idea, especially if you keep a fixed orientation point/cockpit that remains. A good example is the Google spotlight story pearl[49] where the audience takes the same place in a car during the whole journey.

3D 360-degree matchmove

Also, many non-VR productions use camera matchmove. Simply put, some software analyzes your footage, detects features in several pictures and thus is able a) to calculate your exact camera position reversely with a camera solver and b) to identify 3D characteristics of your scene. With this information in 3D software you can integrate (animated) 3D objects to enrich your scene or simply hide the crew and props behind 3D scans of the empty scene. While camera matchmoving for movies with a screen is commonplace today the development of camera matchmoving in 360° VR movies is quite in an early stage. The

---

[49] https://youtu.be/WqCH4DNQBUA

algorithms have to deal with multi lens distortion of your recording that makes the exact feature location in 3D space more difficult. But more and more software offers a solution for this. For example, Nuke (widely known for compositing in 3D space) with its CaraVR plugin demonstrated it at FMX 2017 offering several prebuilt solver nodes. A good starting point if you want to dig deeper into the subject without spending too much money upfront are the Blender 3D based video tutorials "Track, Match, Blend" and "Track, Match, Blend 2" by Sebastian Koenig which to my knowledge doesn't take 360° into account but offer a great foundation with the excellent open source software Blender. You either can buy the courses or get them for free with a monthly subscription fee to the blender cloud[50] (as of May 2017).

Perfect stitching

Today there is no perfect stitching of 360° stereo content without 3D information. And my assumption is that any artificial intelligence solution for feature detection will do a better job if it incorporates depth data (or 3D data). This rule applies to recorded footage with multiple cameras. However, if you completely render your scene, any modern 3D software should be capable of rendering two correct equirectangular stereo spheres which can be used for further processing. In the early days (end of 2014 and during 2015) this was different and I created a half-manual (but automatable) solution which rendered out some (better is one) column of pixels for each eye, rotated both cameras a tiny bit and then rendered the next pixel column. All files were then put together by ImageMagick composing a close to perfect image. However, the render time is way too long in the upper and lower area where you have almost no depth information and the whole resolution width which in your VR headset turns into a single pixel. Addons for your 3D software should provide you with some nice settings e.g. to take this effect into account and blend to a faster render projection. The result should be the same. Of

---

[50] http://cloud.blender.org/

course, you could render your 3D scene with several cameras and later let stitching software do the work for you. But the results of this will probably be poorer than a clean render. The only solution I can think of for this would be to combine real footage with rendered footage.

Let the game engine do the work

One smart thing you can do (and that has been done already) is to put a stereoscopic video recording into a game engine. Cory Strassburger, Kite & Lightning demonstrated this at FMX 2015 in Stuttgart (Did I mention that FMX is a great event?...). My notes from that event state: "cheap way to do 3d acting in VR. greenscreen stereo video of person Then place him on plane orthogonal to camera. This will do."

Let's say I record a stereo movie with two cameras (or my beloved Fuji Real3D which records stereo in HD) in front of a greenscreen. After turning the green to transparent I separate both recordings and throw the videos into my game engine. I have to make sure that the right eye only sees the right recording and the left eye only the left. Especially if this is a moving object like, somebody dancing, the brain will accept it quite as well as a real immersive 3D experience. The game engine provides correct parallax for the rest of the scene. O.K. If I tilt my head too much the stereo impression of the video footage will break. For this reason, it would be better to exchange the second eye video with a depth channel that could distort a grid or mesh and thus provide a real 3D scene with correct parallax. We always come back to the same conclusion: it is better to have a volumetric video turned into an animated mesh to get the best results. This has to be balanced against the performance to be achieved. GPU (graphics processing unit or graphics card) manufacturers and software vendors work on this subject intensively. There is a concept called tesselation (in some areas referred to differently e.g. Micropolygon Displacement in Blender). This reduces the resolution of a 3D render to the maximum resolution of the screen. So, even if your 3D object has more polygons (e.g. by using a subdivision surface modifier), subdivisions and thus render times will be reduced to the screen resolution. It seems the whole world is working on improving the abilities of 3D software and hardware to get real time complex animated 3D into game engines to ease our work as movie makers. So, if you start with a long term project you might want to consider also capturing depth information and 3D data as there may be new ways to process them later. And things are improving here. The first-generation Google Tango phones have a 1cm depth resolution, later generation Tango devices might use the Soli radar chip which increases precision immensely. Refer to this video that demonstrates Google Project Soli[51]. This German article speculates about the usage of radar chips[52]. More rumors that came to my ear led me to expect we will see sensing devices with way higher resolution. This would help low cost real time motion capture for the masses to become reality.

Let the cloud help: render farms and VR streaming

For pre-rendering 360°x180° animations render farms are quite standard today in all animation and VFX productions. It is usual to automate your render tasks and use the distributed power of the web using GPU-based and CPU-based rendering. Large studios often use their own on-premise-hardware or hardware located in a VPN (virtual private network) to keep secret IP separated from the web. Keeping some points in mind may be helpful.

- Do a sufficient amount of testing before throwing large chunks of work on your farm as using your render farm costs you time and money.

- Always take security into account to avoid parts of your work leaking to news websites - or worse - your competitors.

---

[51] https://www.youtube.com/watch?v=0QNiZfSsPc0

[52] https://www.heise.de/ct/artikel/Angetestet-Erstes-Tango-Smartphone-Lenovo-PHAB2-Pro-3234183.html

The Cinematic VR Formula

- Calculate your needs and the break-even for using trusted render farms.

We have seen the streaming of videos and also of games for a while now. One rule of thumb is: the more critical latency is, the harder it gets to use live streaming (which means: the user sends his inputs, the game runs on a remote server, calculates the image and sends it back to the user). While this works well with strategy games or games with low requirements on latency it gets harder with first person shooters where milliseconds can decide whether you are able to sidestep or be killed by a bullet. For VR this is even more challenging. What is of utmost importance is not the latency of the action but the latency of the update frequency when you turn your head wearing a VR headset. Of course, it would be possible to let a streaming farm do the calculation of the whole stereoscopic equirectangular spheres, transfer it to the headset and let the headset choose the correct cropping, but this would be an immense waste of CPU/GPU processing as well as bandwidth as only a small part would be used. Developments of graphic card manufacturers go in the opposite direction as well. They try to render in high detail what is in the center of your view and reduce resolution when it comes to your peripheral vision. Another obstacle (even if computing is superfast) is the distance between the user and the render/streaming farm. The speed of light and electricity is roughly 300,000 kilometers per second. Which means: a signal traveling half way round the globe from Australia to Europe and back (20,000 kilometers each or 40,000 kilometers together at least if not re-routed over satellites) takes 0.1333 seconds which means we could receive 7.5 image updates per second and not 90. So, proximity to your render/streaming farm also plays an important role. But maybe you can find a clever solution using mixed approaches like trajectory forecasting, rendering a bit more than head turning speed allows, render with fewer detail at the borders and a server-farm close to the user. Or a blended approach using local and server resources for different parts of the work. Just keep in mind: the more complex your solution the more likely it is to be a victim of evolving standards.

And as a creative you want to focus on creating a great experience and not configure the latest tech, right?

Conservation and documentation of your assets and processes

As we see this fast evolution of VR movie making, formats and options we have already said that it is vital:

a)   to document everything sufficiently.
b)   to focus on intermediate results as an important layer of your work to be able to re-use it later on for new editions, new formats and new output devices like domes, light field displays, AR headsets, holographic in-air projections, the direct non- invasive brain interface - you name it.

Yes. Both cost additional money. Both are an important investment protection for your work. That may change as visual computing matures. But for now, it is important to reserve budget and time explicitly for this.

Of course, there is a lot more to be done in postproduction But this is also true for ordinary movies and therefore not addressed explicitly here. If you miss something vitally important to VR postproduction that wasn't picked up anywhere else in the book just let me know.

Conclusion

Traditional phases like preproduction, production and postproduction merge and blend together constantly transforming your VR movie production into an iterative process. VR and AR evolve to universal tools from previz to the end-product. VR Analytics and constant extensive user testing also help to iteratively improve your result before you invite your audience to immerse themselves in the final result. And even after starting, VR Analytics might help you to improve your product if you took into account the rules we laid out. With the fast-paced development in the industry the (pre/post)-production process is evolving rapidly. The prepared ones - which includes you of course - will use this velocity to the advantage of their great VR movies. I can't wait to see your amazing results. It is time to move forward to the premiere, to the launch, to box-office-day.

Level 10: - Release Date and Beyond.

"If the boy and girl walk off into the sunset hand-in-hand in the last scene, it adds 10 million to the box office."

George Lucas

Figure 24: Your great VR Movie Release. The producer hands you sacks of money. Paradise..

I assume everything is settled before this day dawns. What I mean is the question of distribution, of the platforms and marketplaces you market your VR movie on or the theaters, planetariums or concert halls and musical locations where you show your masterpiece. If not... oops. This is work that should happen before or during the production process. We didn't cover it because - as I said - it is part of classic game or music projects which you had a look at while reading the books I recommended. You did, didn't you?

So... as I began... Everything is settled for this day. I don't know what your project is. Whether you publish it on steam or have it in a planetarium. Anyway. This is your great day! Enjoy it. Witness the day. Get audience reactions or watch the download counter. It was hard work. Now go and celebrate! You earned it. Take some time off.

The life cycle of your movie

Now the life cycle of your VR movie has just begun. How long will it last and what will happen during and after this life cycle? Well that mainly depends on technology and money.

If your VR movie is a simple or standard format without interaction it can be expected to run pretty well for a long time without any interference being necessary, especially if you use one of the major standard platforms.

But as we have learned, interactive VR experiences are far more attractive. Assuming that you use a game engine your product might be bound to an operating system and a certain version. Also bugs in your product are far more likely so that you have to plan a support phase where you provide patches - at least for the first time of being live. This of course has to be planned upfront as it costs money to provide support and create patches. Maybe you can make a business case for it by planning extension packs to your VR movie, as is common in the games industry.

Also, while planning your movie, already have in mind if you want to create offspring of your main movie or sequels or merchandising or a video game for tablets and smartphones or license the usage of your characters as avatars (if they become popular), or many more things. It does make a difference in your attitude and your results if you produce your masterpiece with this extended plan in mind. It changes your result and the lifecycle of your production. So, think about it early.

Termination of your VR movie

No author wants his book to go out of print. No movie producer wants to experience his movie becoming unavailable. And digital download platforms and on demand services are definitely prolonging the lifetime of many digital goods. But the day of shutdown may come. I don't recommend anything for your mourning process. But I suggest that you keep a copy somewhere so that you can reuse parts of it for later projects and revivals. Nobody knows, but it might happen. Think about Star Wars that took decades to get restored, remastered, extended and continued. Or think about the ancient stereo photographs I found on the web – about one hundred years old. And I was able to reconstruct 3D scenes from them with photogrammetry software that nobody had imagined a century before. Be the archiver, the protector of your masterpieces. Maybe somebody will be grateful that you kept it. Or they might freeze your body, slice and digitize your brain, and reconstruct a virtual world from your movie in which you can reside for thousands of years after the natural death of your body. (This lets us rethink about creating horror experiences, right?) Or it helps to save the world one day - who knows. But those are just some thoughts. It is completely up to you.

GAME OVER - YOU WIN!

I hope you had a great time creating your VR movie and it brought you fame and fortune. Or you learned a lot for your next project. Anyway - you did it. You won. Think about sharing what you learned. It might help people on the journey. I would love to learn what magnificent stuff you create. You are always welcome to drop me a line.

And remember: after the VR movie is before the next VR/AR movie. No matter if you have a multimillion dollar funding or just want to create a piece with nothing: just go out, start small and make something amazing! That is what we all are here for.

Thank you for your company. Also in the name of Player One and Player Two. Hey, do you see this? Player One is nominated for an Oscar for his extraordinary masterpiece and gets handed a sack of gold coins. But where is Player Two? ... Pssst. Do you hear someone mumbling from the trunk of this gangster car? Can't say... they just left and seem to head for the harbor. ... Sorry that I was distracted by this. Thank you, again dear reader. Our journey ends here. **Farewell and have a great time producing awesome VR movies!**

Yours - Chuck Ian Gordon, May 17th 2017 - in the train from Bonn to Frankfurt alongside the beautiful River Rhine, Germany

P.S. To stay informed about the new stuff we do, please take a look at: http://www.cinematic-vr-formula.com or at http://www.GordonsArca.de . Thank you!